Following the Foyle
~ A Portrait of the River Foyle ~

Paintings by Pat Cowley
Text by Ken McCormack

First published by Cottage Publications,
an imprint of Laurel Cottage Ltd.
Donaghadee, N. Ireland 2008.
Copyrights Reserved.
© Illustrations by Pat Cowley 2008.
© Text by Ken McCormack 2008.
All rights reserved.
No part of this book may be reproduced or stored on any media
without the express written permission of the publishers.
Design & Origination in Northern Ireland.
Printed & bound in China.
ISBN 978 1 900935 66 1

Artist and Author

Pat Cowley lives and works in Derry City. He was educated at the Belfast College of Art and the University of Ulster before going into teaching and becoming Head of Art at St. Peters High school in Derry. However as demand grew for his work, Pat moved on to concentrate on his career as a professional artist.

He has had a number of solo exhibitions, with examples of his work and shows to be found in Ireland and further afield in London, New York and Boston. He has also illustrated several books, the most recent one being a book of poetry.

Pat draws his inspiration from the Derry/Donegal hinterland of lakes, rivers, hills and shores and how man interacts with and influences the landscape we inhabit. He also draws much material from the west of Ireland where he combines his art with fly fishing and being in wild unspoilt places.

Ken McCormack is a writer and broadcaster. He was educated at St Columb's College, Queen' University and the University of Ulster. Ken studied for Master's degrees in Education and also in Philosophy and having been a communications engineer changed to teaching. During his career as a lecturer he also joined the BBC as a freelance presenter and documentary maker. Among the programmes he has made are the acclaimed *The Killing of Leitrim* and the celebrated series *Island City* and *North by North West*. He has been a frequent contributor to the *Belfast Telegraph* and currently writes historical sketches for the *Derry Journal*. Ken wrote the supernatural thrillers *The Wednesday Ticket* and *Footsteps* for The Derry Playhouse in 2005 and his new play *On the Subject of Love* will have its premiere at the Playhouse in 2009. He is also awaiting publication of a co-authored non-fiction work and is currently writing a novel to be published in the autumn of 2009. Ken is an avid traveller and his main interests are fitness, drama, literature and music.

Acknowledgements

I could not have undertaken the challenge of writing about the Foyle system without the help of my brother John McCormack, who as a keen amateur historian and fisherman has an intimate knowledge of the Foyle and its rivers. John was a font of information and a constant source of inspiration and guidance. I'd also like to mention my brother Bernard McCormack for his fascinating ideas about rivers and people. Thanks also go to the Strabane historian John Dooher, to the library staff of the Ulster American Folk Park, Central Library in Derry and in the Lifford, Letterkenny and Ballybofey libraries. I'm most indebted to Frank Elliott of Strabane, who with over 60 years experience of fishing the Rivers Mourne and Finn gave me invaluable insights into these rivers. Also, to the many welcoming people that I met along the way – the Gaelic speakers along the Finn; folk from the Isaac Butt Heritage Centre in Glenfinn and Bridgeen Dignan in Ballybofey; also, Andy Patton and the fisherfolk at Sion Mills, and not forgetting the Loughs Agency and the various Angling Associations within the Foyle system. Last but not least to painter Pat Cowley for his skill and patience in conjuring up such magnificent images to complement this portrayal of the great Foyle system.

Ken McCormack 2008

Contents and Illustrations

The Foyle – A Brief Introduction	7
The River Strule	9
Glenock Church near Newtownstewart	16
Foddering sheep in the Glenelly Valley	19
Newtownstewart	23
Night catch on the River	26
The River Mourne	29
The Big Weir at Sion Mills	31
The Swinging Bridge	34
Into a Salmon at the Gravenue	37
Lone Angler on the Mourne	40
The Town of Strabane	43
The River Finn to Ballybofey and Stranorlar	47
The River Finn – the Beginning	46
The Finn – Gathering Strength	49
The Salmon Leap	52
The Sanctuary, the Finn	55
Glenfinn	57
The Finn below the 'Twin Towns'	62

The Finn to the Foyle	63
Beltany Stone Circle, Raphoe	65
The Big Island, below Strabane	72
The River Foyle from Lifford to Derry City	73
The Foyle Valley from Binnion Hill near Lifford	75
Looking across to Port Hall	76
The Foyle at St Johnston	82
The River Foyle from the hills above Carrigans	86
Looking up the Foyle from above the Waterside	88
The Island of Derry	91
Looking up into the city from the Bay Road	95
The city from the Waterside	100
The Docks at Lisahally	102
The River Faughan flowing down from the Eagle's Nest	105
Fishing boats at Quigley's Point	106
Lough Foyle to the Sea	107
The Entrance to the Foyle from Inishowen Head	109
Bibliography	111

The Foyle ~ A Brief Introduction

The river glides on, flowing by for all time.

Horace (Roman poet BC)

When you think about it rivers keep on flowing generation after generation – it's only ourselves that come and go. Rivers serve us in our time as it were – we live with them, we relate to them and I'm sure we sometimes stand in awe of them. Certainly that has been the River Foyle for me. Of course, I should really say the Foyle system, since the great waterway running through the city of Derry is made up of many rivers and streams – 900 miles in all. They flow from the Sperrin and Donegal mountains down two great valleys – gateways in past times for travelling monks, bards, or even marching armies and later still providing natural routes for roads and railways. In the east the Foyle system begins with streams flowing into the River Strule. Eventually the Strule becomes the River Mourne and joins the River Finn coming from Donegal in the west. It is this meeting of the waters that produces the main River Foyle so much associated with Derry and its history.

My plan for the Foyle journey is to trek along as much of the system as possible but also to travel by car where roads offer good panoramas of the surrounding landscape. Drawing all of this together to reflect what makes up the Foyle and the lands through which it flows is an exciting challenge. I am much taken with the notion of river and landscape – river and people. What is to be discovered in these relationships I wonder? What imprints have people left behind? And if rivers have personalities – which, with just a little stretch of the imagination I think they have – then what shall I stumble upon? Perhaps a stream all business-like and anxious to be on its way, or a sullen, moody, lethargic piece of water; maybe I'll chance upon a restful musical waterway, or perhaps one that chatters all day through. I fancy the Foyle system will have all of these – but, the only way to know is to commence the journey and find out.

The River Strule

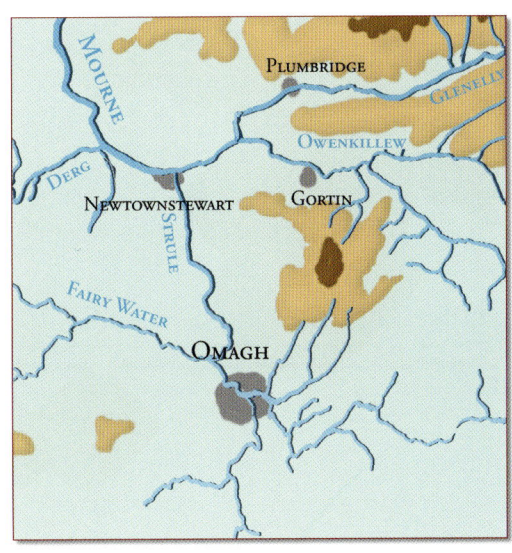

The River Strule (The Stream) is formed with the meeting of the Drumragh and Camowen rivers on the southern outskirts of Omagh town. Technically you could say that these two smaller rivers form the beginning of this part of the Foyle system but since the Strule combines both I feel it provides the best starting point for my journey. The Strule flows through Omagh and launches itself into the countryside in a northerly direction on the way to the main River Foyle and the sea just over 60 miles away. The A5 road follows the course of the River Strule on its left bank from Omagh to Newtownstewart and similarly the A5 continues alongside the River Mourne to Strabane. A secondary road – the B165 out of Newtownstewart follows the right bank of the waterway to Victoria Bridge and thereafter becomes the B72 running all the way to Strabane.

It was the writer Robert Louis Stevenson who said of travelling, *'The great affair is to move'*. So be it, on a winter's day I am moving – the Foyle journey underway. I choose to start

The River Strule

with the River Strule at the oddly named Poe Bridge just a mile or two from Omagh on the Derry road. At this spot the River Fairy Water joins the River Strule and you can see the confluence of the two streams from the bridge – by the way, I tend to use 'river' and 'stream' interchangeably and my dictionary seems happy with that. Anyway, this meeting of the waters is not what you'd call very dramatic for the Strule is already fast flowing and collects the dark meandering Fairy Water in an almost matter of fact way.

It had not escaped me that my old friend the late Alan Warner, Professor of English at the University of Ulster, had come this way on his walking trip around Northern Ireland two decades earlier. Alan, who loved poetry, spotted four swans in a field beside the Fairy Water and quickly penned a couple of lines of verse in his note book:

*'I saw four swans in a field
By Fairy Water…'*

I thought it was a rather beautiful image and I have often wondered did he connect it with the swans of Irish mythology? Unfortunately, we shall never know for it was never mentioned again in any of his poems.

As I survey the scene at the meeting of the Strule and the Fairy Water suddenly I am presented with a puzzle – why is Poe Bridge so named? Here is a mystery and immediately into my mind comes the name of Edgar Allan Poe, the famous writer of weird gothic tales – the spelling of Poe is similar. Yet no one in the locality could throw any light on the question. It was a riddle until I rummaged through my books and came upon a copy of Taylor and Skinner's *Maps of the Roads of Ireland* (1777). And therein lay the answer, for it seems that the Fairy Water and the nearby stretch of the Strule were originally called the River Poe. That surely explained the name of the bridge and I wondered if folks called Poe had once lived here. Certainly it's known that the forebears of Edgar Allan Poe hailed from County Cavan so perhaps other family members had settled in this part of the country in earlier times[*].

Anyway, being almost mid-morning it's time to set out. There are about 12 miles of the River Strule to cover – the town of Newtownstewart, or just below it, being the first destination on this particular stretch of the Foyle journey. The January mid-morning light looks fairly good, with the sun catching the emerald green of the Sperrin Mountains away to the east. Mind you, I see heavy rain clouds gathering rather suspiciously over Bolaght Mountain in the west near the source of the Fairy Water.

The plan is to travel down the right bank of the Strule on foot. This can be accessed from the road to the village of

Cappagh. I can then cross over at Stone Bridge, a distance of about four miles in all. I then join the main road (the A5 – known as the Beltany Road) on the left bank and have a break at the Ulster American Folk Park. Doing this will give me another perspective for having often driven the A5 road I know it provides excellent views of the river on the way into Newtownstewart.

With the journey under way the first thing you notice is that the fairly swift run of the Strule from Omagh to Poe Bridge has become slower. That's because the river having collected the Fairy Water now begins to twist and turn through the countryside. In fact, for a time it all but doubles back on itself like a hairpin bend. At this spot the road to the village of Cappagh (Tilled Land) comes close to the river and it was here that hundreds of salmon were lost due to pollution in August 2004. In normal flow there would be no great depth here and the river width is about forty feet, or thereabouts. Incidentally, attempts were made to speed up this stretch of the Strule by inserting concrete groynes along the river – the hope being that the artificial channels would quicken the flow – and apparently it has helped. Something else of interest here is that the river colour is an intriguing deep brown. This is partly due to the Fairy Water which has meandered through miles of fairly dense peat bog to get to the Strule.

Travelling along the right bank you find 5 lively little burns entering the river. Apart from this, in scenic terms, there's not much relief in the way of trees, bushes, or even vegetation along the Strule. On the opposite side Mountjoy Forest provides a slightly more interesting backdrop but even with this it would be nice to see many more trees on the river bank.

At least I make good progress and as I go I fancy that summer light and shade would greatly enhance the attractiveness of this spot. But it is January – '... *winter-tide, when nothing stirs*' – as the wistful Roman poet Horace puts it. Yet funnily enough something might be stirring on the river bed – freshwater mussels no less. Believe it or not, in times past there was pearl fishing on this stretch. The mussels, which grow in rocky pools, become hosts for the pearls, which are white, fairly small and of no great value. The Strule fishermen – Sligger men as they were called – would use rectangular boxes with glass bottoms to search for clumps of mussels and scoop them out with a cleft stick. Naturally enough there was always the hope that a magnificent specimen would be discovered and make a fortune for someone. Sadly, that cannot happen now, for in a bid to preserve stocks the government introduced a complete ban on mussel fishing some years ago.

The River Strule

Pausing for a little rest provides time to reflect on this business of river journeying. A friend of mine who treks across bogs and clambers up Irish mountains advised me to wear stout waterproof boots and wrap up warm regardless of the season of the year. It's good advice – and after all it is January – I also take something to eat and drink. And certainly one thing you can't be without is a set of Ordnance Survey maps – binoculars are useful too, as is river lore gleaned from local people. The other question is who do you travel with? Samuel Boswell took Dr Johnston, while Robert Louis Stevenson only took his donkey. But the 19th century essayist William Hazlitt insists you must travel on your own – *'Nature is company enough for me. Give me the clear blue sky over my head, and the green turf beneath my feet, and I begin to be myself again.'*

I like this idea of Hazlitt's. It gives you time to reflect, to stop, or go, as you please, to satisfy your curiosity and to consider what is worth recording. And I think this was the way with those gallant folk who've made this journey before me. You see, at least three other travellers have tramped this part of Tyrone and its rivers in the past. The first was John McEvoy at the beginning of the 1800s. He was a self-educated man with skills in forestry, who was chosen by the Royal Dublin Society to carry out the Statistical Survey of the County of Tyrone. Such surveys were published in 1802 for every county in Ireland ostensibly to record agricultural, manufacturing and economic conditions. In reality they covered much more including history, folklore and local circumstances. Reading McEvoy's book I can tell you that in Tyrone the plight of the poor in some localities was unbelievable.

After McEvoy came Dr John Gamble, a man of great insight who, between 1810 and 1820, closely observed country customs in a very philosophic way. It's to Gamble we owe the quote, *'Short sighted persons do not see what others see but they often see what others do not.'*

Then, a few years after Gamble died in 1831, came the third traveller, the redoubtable John O'Donovan. Said to be one the greatest scholars of his time, O'Donovan covered practically every inch of this countryside in the late 1830s as part of the great Irish Ordnance Survey. One of his tasks was to study the meaning of the existing Gaelic place names and to determine a form of spelling suitable for maps – these names are now in every day use. Reading O'Donovan's memoir it appears that he has taken the same route along the Strule as I have – something that gives me great satisfaction as I get underway again.

The trek is about an hour old when Stone Bridge comes into sight. From a distance the 6 arches look pleasing enough – it's nicely symmetrical. But the upper rendering is very

The Ulster American Folk Park

ordinary to say the least of it – and this bridge is really narrow, allowing only single file vehicle traffic. None the less it serves the purpose of crossing to the Strule's left bank and reaching the A5 road just a few hundred yards further on. Not far away you find the neat little village of Mountjoy, and, tongue in cheek or otherwise, I'm told that one of the pastimes in the district is training pigs for races at agricultural shows.

Uppermost in my mind is reaching the Ulster American Folk Park without getting drenched, for rain coming across from west Tyrone is beginning to fall like the proverbial stair rods. It brings me to pondering that favourite saying of the Ancient Greeks – *'Nothing is comparable to water'*. How would they have felt about our winter downpours I wonder? Fortunately, I escape the deluge and lodge myself in the Folk Park's excellent library.

I want to get a feel of what it was like in the Strule valley especially in the days of mass emigration to America. In the past hundreds of folk from these parts would take ship from Derry Quay in the hope of finding a better life in the New World. Luckily enough, I chance upon the autobiography of Thomas Mellon who emigrated to Pennsylvania with his parents in 1818, when he was 5 years of age. In time he was to become entrepreneur, judge and banker – living to the ripe old age of 95. His family home was restored in the

Mellon Homestead

1960s and is situated on the edge of the Folk Park, which was opened in 1976. Here you can visit houses that give you a sense of the Old and New Worlds, see a country Post Office of the 1800s, and climb into the dark recesses of a sailing ship of the time – and there's a lot more in this wonderful archive of past times along the River Strule.

It's just these sorts of imprints that would have registered in the mind of the young Thomas Mellon. He made a return visit to his homestead at Camphill beside the Strule in 1882 and recalled in his book that everything locked in his mind since boyhood was still the same – locations, scenery and of

The River Strule

course the river. That same river still flows past the rear of the Folk Park through a dense piece of woodland, chattering merrily as it goes – a reminder that through all the years of coming and going it is constant, always in touch with the landscape, always there for each generation.

Yet, upon leaving the Folk Park you just get the impression that some sort of change is in the air. On the right bank Cappagh Burn tumbles excitedly in from the Sperrins and suddenly the Strule takes on a new lease of life. The pace of the river quickens as its course straightens and my map indicates that it will keep this run all the way to Newtownstewart. You are much more aware that you are in a valley now, with mountain ranges to the east and to the west. There is more variation in the landscape and more contrast. And despite the fact that it's mid-winter, there's much more in the way of colour in the fields and hillsides – albeit subdued – as the day brightens and the heavy rain shower that nearly soaked me earlier swings away eastwards across the Sperrin range.

After the Folk Park the A5 route follows the course of the Strule very closely. Odd to relate the River Strule used to flow much higher up along the valley but a drop in the level of the sea caused the river to forge a new lower course for itself. You can actually see the old elevated shelves of the early river as you drive on the A5 road. In fact the road lies on one

Heading for Mary Gray

of these shelves and its height allows splendid panoramas of the river and surrounding countryside. Up ahead two ladies lie in wait for me – Bessy Bell and Mary Gray – one on each side of the river. If that sounds somewhat facetious let me tell you that in reality these are two mountains flanking the Strule like sentinels on the approach to Newtownstewart. Bessy Bell (originally Slieve Trim – the Hill of the Elder Trees) is on the left bank of the river, while Mary Gray is on the right bank. At first sight the two seem similar but a closer look reveals quite a few differences. Bessy Bell on the south west end of the Sperrins is a large round topped mountain capped with moorland. It is higher and wider than Mary Gray. On one side there is a set of wind turbines, visible from miles away and on the lower slopes you find neatly manicured rich arable farm land.

Directly behind Bessy Bell and not visible on the approach along the Strule valley is Baronscourt the ancestral home of the Duke of Abercorn. Here since 1612, it boasts magnificent woods, lakes and a game reserve, with wild deer roaming about quite freely. But there are no such luxuries for Mary Gray on the other side of the river. The top looks less rounded than Bessy Bell and certainly the upper slopes are more rugged. I suppose you could say Mary Gray has more of a feel of the Sperrins, which stretch behind to the east, with deep craggy valleys, high summits and backdrops of breathtaking scenery truly reminiscent of Alpine grandeur.

That said, Bessy Bell and Mary Gray are very much part of local folklore, with no end of debate on how the two names came about. The answer probably lies with Scottish settlers who brought a heart-rending ballad to the Strule valley in the 1700s. The story goes that two beautiful girls from Perthshire, Bessy Bell and Mary Gray, locked themselves away in a little house made of rushes to avoid a devastating plague. Each day a youth who loved them brought food until he too caught the disease and then tragically passed it to them. Sadly, all three died, but the tale does not stop in the valley of the Strule – at Staunton in Virginia there are also two hills named Bessy Bell and Mary Gray. You see, when the Ulster Scots left here for America over two hundred years ago one thing they brought with them was the tearful ballad of Bessy Bell and Mary Gray.

Bessy Bell and Mary Gray,
They war twa bonnie lasses;
They built a bower on yon burn-brae,
And they covered it o'er wi' rashes.
But the pest came frae the burrows-town,
And it slayed they baith taegether.

Back to the trek and the Strule swings to the right before turning back towards Newtownstewart, which lies on another hairpin bend in the river barely a mile away. Since the A5 road runs along the valley at a good elevation I pause to take in one of my favourite views for, as I said earlier, I have often travelled this way by car. Just at the intersection of the old route into the town and the new bypass, looking down to the right you see the Strule to the side of a flat green expanse of playing fields. Now if you look carefully back along the river you will see that another stream has entered from an easterly direction. This is the beautiful little Owenkillew River. It flows in smartly from the Sperrins having tumbled down gorges and journeyed through woods of oak, rowan, birch and holly before collecting the Glenelly River just below the village of Plumbridge. Apart from its

The River Strule

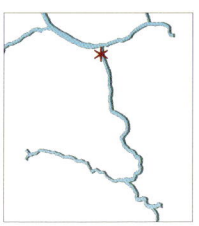

The Meeting of the Waters at Glenock Church near Newtownstewart

popularity with salmon fishermen the Owenkillew has now outdone the Strule in having the largest population of freshwater mussels in Northern Ireland.

By letting the eye wander further to the left you cannot escape the elegant white Glenock Church (St Eugene's R.C.) with its curious wooden spire. I am not sure why but I always associate this church and its surroundings with what you might find in the countryside of New England. The odd thing is that it has a modern look but actually dates to the late 1700s when Catholics were given greater freedom in the practice of their religion. It's believed Glenock Church was the first Catholic place of worship in Ireland to have a belfry – its bell the first post-reformation Catholic bell to ring out across the Irish countryside. And a boast in Newtownstewart is that all traditions came together to build the church – a remarkable act of community good will. Then in 1904 the unusual slim wooden spire, which sets the church off so delightfully, was added.

The road out of Newtownstewart past the church takes you eastwards into the Sperrin Mountains (Na Speirini – Spurs of Rock) and to the little village of Plumbridge. I've already mentioned that the Glenelly River joins the Owenkillew River near here. Both are major contributors to the Foyle system, so I feel a detour – even though it will take another day – is well justified. It's new country for me. The route will take me up the Glenelly Valley into the heart of the Sperrins and I've a reason for going this way. Firstly, I've heard so much about the breathtaking scenery, wildlife and archaeological sites, that I want to see for myself what's available. Secondly, even if it's only for the novelty of it, I would like to try panning for gold – there's big talk about it in these parts. Thirdly, I want to investigate something that happened here 600 years ago when John Colton, Archbishop of Armagh, came through the Sperrins and risked life and limb in a an episode in Derry that matches any medieval mystery.

The first stop is Plumbridge itself – a quiet, out of the way, tidy and pretty little place through which the Glenelly River flows. The bridge here gives its name to the village but you have to take the story of how that came about with a pinch of salt. Apparently, the builder of the bridge over the Glenelly resorted to spitting down into the river in order to get the correct plumb, or vertical alignment. From that time the village growing around the river became known as Plumbridge. The bridge looks fine to me and I suppress a smile as I consider it can't have been a windy day during that unusual method of construction all those years ago.

Not far from Plumbridge is the tiny village of Cranagh, where you find the Sperrin Heritage Centre, which has fine exhibits covering the geology and culture of the area. At

The River Strule

this stage the Glenelly River looks not much more than a little stream as it weaves its way along the floor of the steep-sided valley into the heart of the Sperrins. To the left are the twin mountains of Sawel and Dart – Sawel is the highest in the range but both are visible from miles away and are often regarded as flagships for the beauty of the Sperrins when they turn deep purple in the summer. A common trend hereabouts is that hills have the prefix Mullagh, which means mound, or summit, and you can see that in the many rounded hilltops sitting out against the skyline and clothed in heather and gorse. In the valley below you find copses and thickets on the river banks, and sprinkled about too are forests of conifers and clumps of deciduous trees such as oak and ash.

There's a patchwork of small fields with hedgerows and stone fences on the lower slopes above the Glenelly River and it looks fertile land to me – the intense emerald green luminosity of the pastures positively glows in the sunshine. I notice in several places that there are neatly spaced sets of ridges concealed under the grass and I've been on the lookout for these features. They are called Potato Rigs or Lazy beds. This was a quick method of getting the best out of a small patch of land in pre-famine days of the early 1800s. The sod was turned over with a spade called a loy. Then the potato tubers were inserted and the sod put back in place. The loy had a special shape for the job and I recall Pegeen's strange line in Synge's *Playboy of the Western World* about the virtues or otherwise of *'the blow of a loy spade…'*

Given the vast, untamed expanse of the Sperrins it's not surprising to find wildlife in abundance. The majority of smaller Irish birds breed here – finches, thrushes, blackbirds, yellow hammers and many more. There are skylarks aplenty and several species of bats, and birds of prey such as hawks, falcons and buzzards are a common sight. The Sperrins even had a visit from one of the Golden Eagles released in Glenveagh Park in County Donegal not that long ago. On the ground especially at night time, you'll see foxes, badgers and hedgehogs in good numbers. The Irish hare, which is almost white in winter and turns reddish brown in summer, is also to be seen. It's now a protected species and loves romping in the meadows, bogs and open land of the Sperrins. I'm not in the least surprised to find that the great arc of the Sperrins between Derry and Tyrone (5,452 sq. miles) has been declared an Area of Outstanding Natural Beauty. Add to this the range of archaeological sites spread across the area – tombs, dolmens, standing stones and stone circles and you have a paradise for families, groups and individuals, wishing to explore the great outdoors.

If you get tired of seeing the sights you can turn your hand to prospecting for gold. Don't expect anything like the Californian or Alaskan Gold Rush, but there is gold in the Sper-

Glenelly Valley

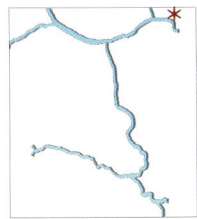

Foddering Sheep in the Glenelly Valley

The River Strule

rins. It's found in the seams of local quartz and eventually turns up in the streams – thus the name alluvial gold, which you can pan for. Like everything else there's a knack to it and you can find out more at the Sperrin Heritage Centre. You use what's termed a gold pan – not made of gold of course, but it may be of metal or plastic, green being the preferred colour. A typical pan might be about two and a half inches deep, sixteen inches wide at the top and around ten inches at the bottom. With your pan filled with water, sand and gravel from a stream, you thoroughly mix the contents with a vigourous movement. Then you wash the mixture off in little waves so that the heavier gold particles fall to the bottom of the pan. Simple as that sounds I can tell you it's an acquired skill and, while I've nothing to show for my efforts, the whole process of panning for gold is highly satisfying.

Before taking leave of the Sperrins I reflect that the upper reaches of the Glenelly Valley eventually lead to mid-Ulster. This brings me to something I mentioned earlier – the saga of John Colton and Derry. In the annals of Ireland it has come to be known as Archbishop Colton's Visitation to Derry – a mission that nearly ended in disaster. In autumn 1397 Archbishop John Colton travelled from Armagh to Derry by way of ancient paths here in the Sperrins. As Primate he had serious business on hand. Now you might think this is dry history but it's not, for the Colton trip was dangerous and provocative and in the end incredible intrigue and corruption was uncovered in the monastery of Derry.

Colton was an English man of Norman extraction appointed to the See of Armagh in 1382. These were times when the Irish Church was still settling into the strictures of the diocesan system after hundreds of years of Celtic independence from Rome. Popes of the time relied heavily on England to keep the situation under control. As for Colton, although he believed Armagh was owed money from church lands in the north west of Ireland, the real object of his Visitation was to restore the Church's crumbling authority in Derry.

Colton's party left Armagh early in October 1397 and made for mid-Ulster. From here they entered the Sperrins, taking routes that depended on landmarks, rivers and valleys. The entourage was impressive – fifteen clergymen and as many clerks, servants and guards – in the middle of it all Colton, suitably attired in his crimson Primate's robes. They rode and they walked according to the state of the terrain, fearful of every step taken, for even church folk were fair game amongst some of the warring clans. Then at last they came alongside Mullaghcarn, a mountain at the head of Gortin Glen in the south east of the Sperrins. This tells us that they were making for the Owenkillew Valley. It runs below Gortin Glen roughly parallel with the Glenelly Valley and is no great distance from the village of Cappagh. In doing so

Dipper at Gortin

they were hoping to get a firm fix on their whereabouts and also suss out the state of affairs on the approaches to Derry. After Cappagh they set off along the River Strule in much the same direction as I take myself.

Now you may wonder how we know all of this. The answer is that every step of the way was recorded in diary form by Colton's good friend Richard Kenmore, a priest and brilliant lawyer. Remarkably, the original manuscript, written over 600 years ago, still exists and is kept in the Republic of Ireland archives. It is an invaluable record of the early Church in Ireland. From it we learn that Colton's diplomacy and his nerve was to be severely tested in the coming days. One thing he knew as he gazed into the River Strule

was that the word would already be out all the way to Derry – the Archbishop of Armagh, a Sasanach (Englishman), was coming to put his nose into their business.

But for the moment we shall leave John Colton on the banks of the river pondering his next move. Little would he have known then that the spot where he was standing would in future times be the busy little town of Newtownstewart, which was built by William Stewart in 1619 during the Plantation. The ruin of Stewart's castle – a manor style dwelling – sits at the end of the main street, having been burned by the retreating troops of James II on the way back from the Siege of Derry in 1689.

Later, in more peaceful times during the 1700s, Newtownstewart became a staging post for travellers on the way to and from Derry. This increasing traffic brought one of the first bridges over the Strule – a sturdy, narrow, 6-arch structure. It was built in 1727 and is still in use today. Up until 1795 most of the Derry Fly-Coach traffic to Dublin went by Armagh – an arduous two day journey. But all of that was to change with the introduction of the famous Bianconi stagecoaches in 1805, when a daily service was commenced between Derry and Dublin via Newtonstewart.

One landmark the stagecoach travellers would have spotted on the south west skyline above the town was Harry

The River Strule

Avery's Castle – an early Irish fortification constructed of stone. All that remains now are twin semi-circular towers that look quite Norman in style to me. But, this place holds a strange yarn that I shudder to tell you. You see, Harry Avery is the Anglicised version of Henry Aimbreidh O'Neill – a local chieftain (b 1392), who had a sister so ugly that no one dared to look upon her. I hesitate to say but her features were somewhat pig-like in appearance. Be that as it may, Harry was intent on finding a match for her and he offered a huge dowry if a suitable husband could be found. The story is told that when the suitors stepped forward they drew back in horror at the sight of the poor girl. Harry's response was to hang each man who refused her hand and if you can believe it, 19 men, or more, went to the gallows in the castle perched high on the hill above Newtownstewart.

There is yet one other gory tale to tell before we take our leave of this town on the Strule. It is a story that made national headlines as The Newtownstewart Murder and in my way of reckoning must surely ring a bell with Agatha Christie buffs. In June 1871 William Glass, a bank clerk who had moved from Derry to the Northern Bank in Newtownstewart, was found murdered. He had been brutally beaten about the head and £1600 of the bank's money was missing. The local police inspector Thomas Hartley Montgomery was called in to investigate and set about questioning people. But, during his enquiries someone pointed out that he himself had been seen in the vicinity of the bank near the time of the murder. Montgomery dismissed this saying he had been visiting Glass, who was a good friend of his. Then, some of the missing money was found nearby and incriminating evidence led to Montgomery's arrest for the murder of the bank clerk. In all it took two years to convict him and he went to the gallows during a thunderstorm in Omagh the like of which had never been seen. Thomas Hartley Montgomery was calm throughout, having spent his last few hours writing philosophic letters to his friends back in Newtownstewart and Derry.

As the Strule bids goodbye to Newtownstewart you are aware of the neatness of the farms and also the number of small rounded hills on each side of the river – perhaps hummocks would be a better description. These are drumlins. Experts say they were formed by a great glacier that once occupied the valley all the way down to the ocean. One thing they do is to cause tremendous variation in light and shade when the sun shines, so that the variety of green hues across the countryside is staggering – especially where they merge into the blue and purple haze over the Donegal hills in the distance.

Equally pleasing is the wooded nature of the banks along the Strule below Newtownstewart. For me, trees, or even bushes, add much more character to any space and especial-

Newtownstewart

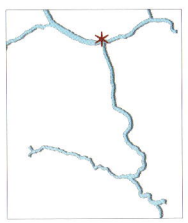

Newtownstewart

The River Strule

ly so to rivers. Long after the Ice Age but before Celtic times it seems there was a great oak wood stretching all the way from here to Derry. You will still find oaks but our other native trees such as beech, sycamore, ash and willow are much to the fore now. Another nice thing is that you can enjoy the sight of the Strule and its tree-lined banks when travelling by car since the new bypass runs alongside the river beyond Newtownstewart.

Yet after a few miles change is in the air again for without warning another stream comes in from the west on the Strule's left bank. This is the River Derg (The Red One), and it enters the river at right angles without much fuss. There is just one thing as we shall presently see – this confluence marks the end of both the Strule and the Derg – from here a much bigger river appears in the Foyle system.

But before leaving the River Derg, a few words about the many traditions to be found along its banks. The river itself flows out of Lough Derg in County Donegal. Making its way through the hills the Derg then meanders along a broad vale collecting the Glendergan and Mourne Beg rivers and countless burns before it meets the Strule. Barely a mile up stream on the Derg you find Ardstraw (The Height Above the River Holm), a tranquil little village much associated with St Eugene in the 6th century, when it was home to a community of monks.

Ardstraw was once a bishopric and remained an important parish in the 14th century. No surprise then that this is where we next find Archbishop Colton's party stopping the night after travelling down the Strule's left bank in that autumn of 1397. A large group of villagers turned out to welcome them. They were entertained regally and guards were placed outside their lodgings during the night. The following day the party was given fresh horses and food and informed that the friendly stopovers on the way to Derry were Urney and Leckpatick parishes. The journey would first take them down river and then they would turn west along the old path to Urney (Place of Prayer) on the River Finn. Failing mishaps they would make Derry – Doire Columcille (Columcille's Oak Wood) by nightfall the following day. The people of Ardstraw walked with them for a short distance and as they made their goodbyes on the river bank Colton commenced turning his mind as to how he might deal with the hazardous situation in Derry.

Apart from Colton, Ardstraw was a stopover for the countless pilgrims coming and going to St Patrick's Purgatory at Lough Derg, as was Castlederg some five miles further upstream. Castlederg is now a busy market town – the most westerly in Northern Ireland. Travellers from all over Europe passed through Castelderg from the 12th century onwards. However, the early settlement was frequently destroyed by in-fighting between the local O'Neill and O'Donnell chief-

tains. Indeed the castle, which gives the town its name, was originally an ancient Irish construction. Later it was rebuilt during the Plantation of Ulster. Did Davy Crockett, who was dubbed 'King of the Wild Frontier', and later killed at the battle of the Alamo, have Castlederg connections? He was born in America but there's a strong tradition that some of his forebears hailed from around here and nearby Donegal.

About 5 miles further upstream in the direction of Lough Derg you come to the village of Killeter, which, despite its remoteness, has found fame well beyond the borders of County Tyrone thanks among other things to the song *Killeter Fair*. It's attributed to farm labourer Francis Kelly, who in the early 1900s penned lines about a beautiful maid he'd spotted at the fair:

> *She stole my heart completely, boys*
> *The truth I must declare*
> *And the first place that I met her*
> *Was at Killeter Fair.*

Yet there's more to Killeter than just the well-known song. At a wedding in the village in the 1930s the best man married the bride — accidentally, of course. It seems the bride-to-be arrived at the church to find her future husband and the best man waiting with grins as big as Cheshire cats. To put it politely they'd been overdoing the celebrations. When the minister asked the bridegroom to respond to the wedding vows he became confused and tongue-tied. Ever the stalwart, the best man made the replies and, believe it or not, was officially married to the girl. The mistake was only discovered at the signing of the register — to the minister's horror it must be added. Thankfully all was put to right, for a new ceremony was held straight away and the young couple were properly wed without any further mishap.

Killeter Fair used to be held in the village each month and was a great meeting place for country people and naturally there were yarns aplenty — happily it's been revived. Some folk relate how there's a fortune in gold sovereigns buried in a local hill since the late 1700s. It was hidden there in a foal's skin by one of Ireland's famous highwaymen Proinsias Dubh (Black Frank McHugh). The story goes that as a youth Proinsias met a pirate at Killeter Fair and was persuaded that there were good pickings to be had from the rich. Soon, he had amassed thousands of gold coins and he marked the hiding place by lining up the church steeple with the last ray of the setting sun on the nearby hill in mid-June. With those directions no need to tell you the fortune has never been found. But I suppose if you believe there was a pirate at Killeter Fair then anything's possible.

The River Strule

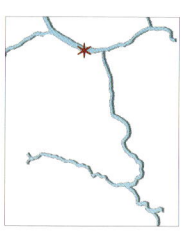

Night catch on the River

Confluence of the Derg and the Strule

One stronger belief is that St Patrick travelled down the valley of the Derg through Killeter after visiting Purgatory on Station Island in Lough Derg. And that brings us to the colour red as suggested in the name Derg (Dearg-Red). Legend has it that the blood of the last great serpent in Ireland slain by St Patrick coloured the waters of the lough and also of course the River Derg, which flows out of it. Perhaps a trifle less romantically, others say that the bed of the river used to contain deposits of red earth and this accounted for the colour of the water in early times. As for myself looking at the Derg where it meets the Strule I can only see the familiar rich peaty brown so typical of streams that come from the mountains of Ireland.

Another thing that occurs to me while standing at the confluence of the two rivers is that this is the third meeting of the waters I've encountered on the journey down the valley from Poe Bridge outside Omagh. Thinking about it the Fairy Water and the Derg join the Strule more or less at right angles so they are somewhat dominated by the main stream. However, the Owenkillew at Newtownstewart comes in at a sharper angle and having been tumbling down from the Sperrins has more dash and freshness about it.

Nonetheless, quiet, or lively, I have to say that there's something magical about the meeting of the waters. In the Vale of Avoca it inspired Thomas Moore to write a famous song and in India the confluence of rivers has great spiritual significance. For me, it's a union of energies from different places – mountains, valleys, forests, wild terrain, villages and towns – and I wonder if the rivers and streams of the Foyle system had voices what tales would they tell about the countryside they flow from?

Anyway, having completed the first stage of the journey what do I make of it all? On reflection I find the Strule to be a river of contrasts – the nature of landscape influences each particular stretch. Below Poe Bridge the river is somewhat bland and lethargic. I feel it tends to get lost in the countryside. But further downstream towards Newtownstewart with the arrival of the Owenkillew the Strule suddenly becomes a busy river and is quite dramatic against the backdrop of the Sperrin foothills. Overall my impression is one of a river-country relationship – there is not one weir, or mill race, or any sign of the Strule having been put to work. The reason for this is that it would have needed a major project in past times to go to the trouble of damning the river given its width and volume. Instead, you find that smaller operations, such as corn, spade and scutch mills, were located along the more manageable streams flowing into the Strule. And so the river is left to interact with its natural surroundings – much to the benefit of the wildlife, the beautiful surrounding countryside and, of course, the

The River Strule

fishermen, for this river, like the whole system, is famed far and wide for its salmon fishing.

* Note Poe Bridge. Since completing this stretch of the journey I have discovered that three Poe brothers William, Thomas and Anthony, came from England and took land in Tyrone during the Plantation (1620). Family members also had property in Fermanagh, Donegal, Cavan and King's County (Cork). The name Poe may relate to a name for the peacock, or possibly be derived from another family name Poer; but some believe it comes from the House of Po (Near the River Po) in Italy. John and Jane Poe of Dring, Co Cavan, were the grandparents of the famous writer Edgar Allan Poe. John came from Donegal and Jane from Ballymoney.

The River Mourne

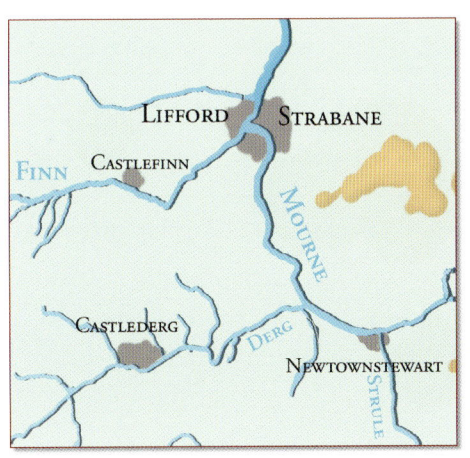

After swinging to the right from the confluence the River Mourne finds itself in a hairpin bend to the left. From here it takes a straight run into the village of Sion Mills, where for the first time since leaving Omagh the river flow is controlled by weirs and sluices to provide waterpower for mill operations. Below Sion Mills the river runs more or less straight all the way into Strabane. The A5 road continues to follow the course of the River Mourne on the left bank all the way to Strabane, while the B165 secondary road runs along the left bank and is replaced by the B72 after Victoria Bridge.

The River Mourne comes into being with the meeting of the Strule and the Derg and it also marks the beginning of the second stage of the journey. I opt to take the second class road out of Newtownstewart (B165), which follows the river on its right bank. This route is elevated and offers good views of the country on the far side of the Mourne. According to an old friend, the late Jim Bradley – renowned histo-

The River Mourne

rian of the Strabane area – Mourne was originally Morne, and most likely was the name of a De Danann prince. Anyway, a bright spring-like January day sees me underway and I must say the winter colours please me greatly, much more subdued than summer hues as I noted the day before but pleasant with it, and the low sun lends a burnished coppery hue to the landscape. A mile or two downstream you find the conically-shaped and quaintly named Gillygromes Hill and nearby is the tiny village of Douglas Bridge, where some lines of verse I'd once heard come to mind;

> *On Douglas Bridge I met a man,*
> *Who lived adjacent to Strabane.*
> *"God save ye, Sir," I said with fear,*
> *"You seem to be a stranger here."*
> *"Not I," said he, "nor any man*
> *Who rides with Count O'Hanlon."*

It's a haunting tale of bygone days – Cromwellian times – when young Tyrone gallants found their refuge in the hillsides hereabouts with their leader Count O'Haloran. No doubt the Mourne was little different then from what it is now, a meandering stream, which now straightens itself after a mile, or so, on the way past the village of Victoria Bridge.

Victoria Bridge had a Nestle's chocolate factory in the 1960s and used cocoa beans brought in from Trinidad. The village got its name on the map thanks originally to the Londonderry and Enniskillen Railway (1847) – one of the first in Northern Ireland. People hereabouts will tell you the railway station was unique in that it was beautifully finished in wood. There was also a narrow gauge tram track to Castlederg seven miles away, so you can imagine that back in the early 1900s Victoria Bridge must have been a real hive of activity with folks travelling to and from Strabane and Derry.

One thing has already been striking me on this stage of the journey – there is now some evidence of activity along the river – what I referred to earlier as the relationship between the river and people. You see this at Victoria Bridge where the course of the river along the valley attracted the railway in the mid-1800s and as result a sizeable community sprang up here. But as yet there is no sign that the river itself was put to use – that, I know, lies up ahead for my map indicates that the village of Sion Mills famous for flax-spinning – is just a over a mile downstream and can be reached by the Camus Road out of Victoria Bridge.

Camus (Cam Uisce) means crooked water, or as it is here – bend in the river. The Mourne does bend considerably to the left now and I spot two bridges spanning the river – Breen's Bridge and Camus Bridge – one on each side of the bend. Both are remnants of the old GNR railway line from Derry.

Sion Mills

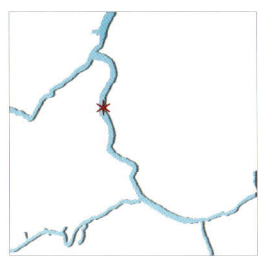

The Big Weir at Sion Mills

The River Mourne

A laneway affords access down to Camus Bridge, which although somewhat dilapidated is a memento of solid Victorian engineering. Quite a few of these bridges were built all along the valley across bends in the river to keep the railway route as straight as possible on the way to Omagh. But it is at Camus Bridge that I am overtaken by what I can only say is something akin to déjà vu – an overwhelming sense that I have been here before. Then it strikes me that it's true, but only in the sense that I had often travelled over this bridge as a child on family holidays to Dublin. In those days it was a long haul – a five hour journey from the GNR railway station in Derry to what was then Amiens Street Station (Now Dublin Connolly) at the other end. I can still remember the names of the stations on the way and the bridges stood out since there was always a rhythmical hollow clunk as the train made its way across. Yet it's strange how for a single moment the countryside around here suddenly becomes familiar to me.

Back to the Mourne and it's intriguing to discover that the world famous hymn writer Cecil Francis Alexander had great affection for this part of the river at Camus. Tradition has it that two lines in *All things Bright and Beautiful* were written here:

> 'The purple-headed mountains,
> The river running by…

The river no doubt is the Mourne and one of the purple-headed mountains is thought to be Bessie Bell in the south – mind you, some say it's Meenashesk to the east. CFA, as her friends called her, lived for a time in the Camus-juxta-Mourne rectory, which overlooks the river from the right bank. Her husband William, later to become Protestant Bishop of Derry and then Primate of Ireland, was appointed to the parish in 1860. So CFA could gaze down at the river from her window.

However, my own feeling is that she wrote the hymn when living with her parents in the exquisite Milltown House a little further downstream – this would have been long before she was married. Her father, Major Humphries, had come from Wicklow to be agent for the Marquis of Abercorn at Baronscourt. So the girl would often have strolled along the river bank and it was her keen sense of everything around her that eventually led in 1848 to the outstanding book *Hymns for Little Children* that went to sixty-nine editions. I've not the slightest doubt that CFA was an outstanding religious poet. Her beloved husband William was said to have been the greatest orator ever heard at Oxford and given their historic connection with Derry we'll be hearing more of the Alexanders before this Foyle journey is over.

As the gifted girl was busy penning her hymns I'm sure she was aware of the huge building operations taking place on

Sion Mills

Herdman's Mill

the River Mourne's left bank – looking across she would have seen the beginnings of the famous Sion Mills. By the 1840s a massive stone weir stretched across the river's full width – all of 130 feet at this particular spot. To the side a water course, or mill race, was excavated to a width of 35 feet and a depth of 6 feet and stout sluice gates were erected to control the flow to 2 giant water wheels that drove the mill. Behind this were buildings in various stages of construction and a little further back a village comprising rows of neat cottages was taking shape. All of this was the brainchild of the Herdman brothers James, John and George, in 1835. They aimed to establish one of the world's great flax-spinning enterprises in a setting which would give prime consideration to their workforce. It was more or less based on the notion of work, rest and play, and of course pray must also be added – very much a Victorian ethic.

To achieve all of this, alongside the mill they constructed a model village with provision for worship, education and recreation. An outstanding feature of the setting was the inclusion of red tiled, half-timbered, mock Tudor buildings that added rustic charm to the whole environment. This idea was introduced by the architect William Unsworth, who was James Herdman's son-in-law. Unsworth designed the first theatre at Stratford-upon-Avon and was said to have an eccentric approach bordering on fantasy. This probably also accounts for the delightful Byzantine style Church of the Good Shepherd in the heart of Sion Mills village. Also in the Unsworth Tudor style is Sion House – a half-timbered mansion with pepper pot chimneys. Set amongst lawns, gardens and exotic trees, it looks as if it is straight out of the Cotswolds in England. Generations of the Herdmans grew up here and a regular visitor was the renowned song writer Percy French – afterwards also acclaimed for his painting.

The River Mourne

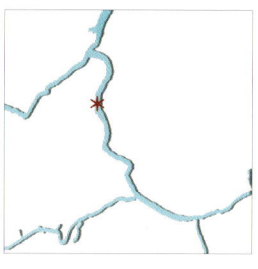

The Swinging Bridge

One of the Herdmans recalled how as a child Percy French took a large dinner plate and drew a picture on it with dripping wax from a burning candle. Unfortunately, when the family went searching for the memento they found a servant had washed the plate in hot water and to everyone's consternation the unusual painting had melted away.

By the way, Sion is not the biblical Sion – the name derives from Shean meaning the Fairy Mound, or Fairy Mount. When the Herdmans decided to put their great idea into practice they looked at Ballyshannon in County Donegal and then visited existing mill works at Seein (Shean) beside the River Mourne. Two features – the quality of the local flax and the potential horsepower of the river – left the Tyrone location the clear winner and in this way Sion Mills as we know it came into being.

That was a hundred and seventy years ago and sadly production at Sion Mills has now ceased. However, the Sion Mills Buildings Preservation Trust has been making progress with a plan to reinvigorate the whole mill area – already, the great chimney, a landmark for miles around at a height of 135 feet – has been restored, and amongst a range of projects preparations are being made to develop workspace units. I'm given the opportunity to visit this vast complex, which is dominated by the main mill – a four-storey building in yellow coloured brick and sandstone very much Italianate in style with its handsome tower. Yet the whole place is rather desolate – there's a great feeling of emptiness all around. Inside you see floor after floor of rusting machinery – an indication of how fickle the world's shifting economy is – China does the bulk of this work nowadays. I try to imagine of the noise and the clamour that once was here, the hundreds of workers, the gossip, the stories and the characters young and old – regrettably, the last of this tide of human energy drained away in 2004 with the mill's closure.

To the river again and you cross from the right bank to the mill via what is known locally as the Swinging Bridge – officially it's called the Bearley Bridge because of the little village nearby. This is a suspension bridge built in 1988 after its predecessor was washed away – apparently it's a common fate of bridges at this spot, though the existing structure is high and sturdy. The crossing here was originally provided to enable the workers to come over from the right bank to the mill but these days it's mainly used by ramblers and fishermen.

Now if I was to choose a favourite viewing area for the River Mourne at Sion Mills it would be at the weir on the left bank at the start of the mill race. Here, you are more or less on the tip of a little island. Facing downstream the weir and the river is to the right and the mill race is to the left. The water is brown and foaming over the weir but it has not the rich

The River Mourne

dark appearance of the slower runs further upstream. Just below here the river is all of a hundred feet across and fishermen can wade most of it with care. Indeed, the Mourne is said to be one of Europe's great salmon rivers – and the run known as the Gravenue, which is joined by a burn of similar name is one of the most popular. People come from across the world to fish at Sion as they do throughout the whole Foyle system and along the river there are privately owned fishing stretches as well as many other fishing spots for clubs and tourists at regular intervals.

As for the mill race, or lade (a Scottish word), it is the widest and swiftest I've ever come across. Suddenly you realise why the Herdmans were attracted to the River Mourne. One of the first things you notice is a system of sluices, massive cog wheels and vertical lifting machinery that would gladden the heart of any industrial archaeologist. Here the water gurgles and swishes – the French poet Rimbaud likened the sound to whispering – before being sucked under the sluice and escaping into the mill race proper, where it dashes off at a staggering pace and is then diverted into the mill to drive the turbine. In early times the turbines provided power for the factory and also light for the village. These days new equipment enables the electrical energy to be fed into the Northern Ireland grid system. Finally, the mill race is channelled back into the river below the Swinging Bridge and it seems to me the course is much rockier along this lower stretch.

The month being January it's not the time for rod and line here. Yet I meet a fisherman looking pensively at the river and obviously longing for the start of the new season. During our chat he's able to tell me how some of the favourite pools on the River Mourne got their names – Purgatory Pool is one where the fish cannot move upstream when there's low water so they have to do a spell of time there – it appears the fish can go into a mighty frenzy if there's no sign of rain. It's hard to believe in these days of fancy swimming pools and spas that swimming used to be a fairly regular activity in most rivers. At Sion the Nude Pool was where the young men of the village kept cool, or learned to swim, or even washed themselves in bygone days when it seems summers were much warmer. And I want to know about another spot with a curious name – the Lord Pool. This apparently relates to a tragedy on the Mourne in times long past. The story goes that in June 1655, twenty-two year old James Hamilton, Third Lord Strabane, got into difficulties and drowned in the Mourne while fleeing from Cromwellian soldiers – he had been brought up a Catholic and was a supporter of the Royalist cause. Thus the Lord Pool still reminds us of his fate three and half centuries later.

Sion Mills

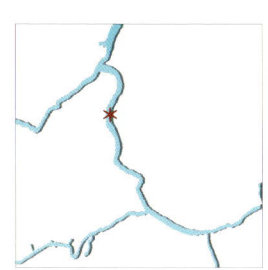

Into a Salmon at the Gravenue

The River Mourne

I could not leave Sion Mills without a mention of its legendary status in the annals of cricket. It's been played in the village since 1865. Ireland defeated the West Indies at Sion on 2 July 1969 having bowled them out for 25 runs in the first innings. The cricket ground lies in the shadow of the mill right beside the Mourne and whether it was the dreamy tranquillity of the river setting, or Irish hospitality the night before, the great Test side crumbled to leave Ireland with a proud result in the history of cricket. My first ever visit to this exquisite ground was when our schoolboy team came to play against Sion lads in a summer long ago. The railway from Derry to Belfast (and Dublin) was along one of the boundaries and a canny old spectator in a straw hat and blazer said to me – "If you hit the ball out of the ground into a wagon when the train is passing it'll be the longest 6-hit in cricket". Jokingly, he meant that the ball would travel all the way to Belfast. I never managed that, but I often returned to Sion Mills to play cricket and became great friends with many of the talented players there who went on to play for Ireland – it has left me with treasured memories.

After Sion Mills the Mourne runs a fairly straight course to Strabane about three miles away. I stop briefly at Ballyfatton at the site of the Lord Pool and find the river to be deep and swift. The land is gently hilly on the left bank, while on the right bank you see the last of the western Sperrins – Meenashesk, rises to about a thousand feet, while downstream

Cricketers

Knockavoe Hill sits above Strabane somewhat less in height. By taking the back road into the town on the right bank you come to Milltown House, now Strabane Grammar School. As mentioned already this was formerly the home of Cecil Frances Alexander. Apart from the magnificent house, CFA's daughter, Eleanor, has left a description of what the surroundings were like in the mid-1800s –

'There was a glen beside the house - a haunt of delight, through which ran a stream, with little waterfalls and a sinister pool. At the bottom was a rat-infested mill and a surly white-faced miller.'

Strabane

The stream was the Cavanalee River, which still runs into the Mourne, and the glen, known locally as Patten's Glen, has recently been landscaped with the addition of hazel and ash trees.

Barely a mile upstream along the Cavanalee River is the townland of Dergalt (The Red Glenside) and here you find the ancestral home of President Woodrow Wilson – one of twelve presidents with Ulster ties. His grandfather James trained at Gray's printing press in Strabane and emigrated to America in 1807 at the age of twenty. A talented young man, James became a newspaper editor, then a judge and finally a member of the US Senate. It was his son Joseph who was the father of President Wilson – 28th President of the United States. The Wilson home is now under the care of the National Trust. A wonderful example of an Irish cottage of the late 1700s, it has been preserved exactly as it was in the days of Woodrow Wilson's grandfather.

Having collected the Cavanalee River the Mourne straightens its course and flows through the centre of Strabane. The town lies at the north western tip of the Sperrins and is bisected by the river, with buildings and houses clustered on the low ground of the right bank. Gradually, with the passage of time, the surrounding slopes have seen developments that make the whole setting very pleasing – especially with the spires of the two churches against the skyline. Personally speaking I have always regarded Strabane as a fine town, rich in history and tradition, and very much linked with nearby Lifford just over the border in the Irish Republic. Strabane (Fair Valley River, or White Holm) has seen its fortunes vary from days of great prosperity to times of serious unemployment. It is in an ideal position to be a market town being on the route from Derry to Omagh and close to Donegal, but economic fluctuations have brought good times and bad times in equal measure.

Although there were settlements of the O'Neill and the O'Donnell clans from early times around Strabane it was not until the Plantation that it began to take shape as a town. James Hamilton, First Earl of Abercorn in Scotland, was appointed as the principal undertaker for the area and in 1612 he commenced building a castle, houses and a church. Thus began the long association with the Abercorns and the Strabane area – one which saw substantial commercial development and sometimes friction as well.

 In the beginning they set up a ferry to provide a river crossing but expansion and through traffic to Dublin eventually necessitated a bridge. A later venture supported by John James Hamilton 9th Earl of Abercorn in the late 1800s was the building of the Strabane Canal. This took boats from the River Foyle right into the heart of the town at Canal Basin and operated until the early decades of the 1900s – it

The River Mourne

Lone Angler on the Mourne

Strabane

was in effect a little port. You can still see the clear outline of Canal Basin, which these days has the shape of a wide square. Its now partly a car park but one or two of the old warehouses that surrounded the Basin are still standing.

Strabane grew rapidly as a market town and a centre for linen in its early days but one of the most enterprising aspects was the development of printing. The town became a leader in publishing throughout Ireland, with at least ten commercial printing presses in the 1700s. Strabane also had one of the first newspapers in the country.

And one of the town's printing houses – Gray's – was to become world famous. Apart from James Wilson of Dergalt, who was an apprentice there, Gray's Printing Press in Strabane is linked with John Dunlap who printed the American Declaration of Independence. John worked in Gray's as a boy before joining his uncle's printing business in Philadelphia in 1757. Soon Dunlap got to know the founders of American's fledgling administration – he would have been friendly with people like Benjamin Franklin and Thomas Jefferson. Then, on 4 July 1776, he was asked to print the first draft of the epoch making Declaration, which contained the forever memorable words *'We hold these truths to be self-evident, that all men are created equal…'* Afterwards, John Dunlap went on to publish America's first daily newspaper and became a very rich man for quite often he was paid in real estate rather than money.

I call at Gray's Printing press in Main Street Strabane – the original bow front window with its bull's eye glass is still preserved and it's a most striking frontage. Inside is an Alladin's Cave of printing memorabilia, including three early printing presses still in working condition. It strikes me that both young Dunlap and Wilson would have seen the River Mourne day and daily from Gray's windows – there would have been few buildings to block the view in their times. And no doubt they would have played and sported themselves along the river bank as well. They were never to return but I'm sure both of them kept a picture of the Mourne in their memories since it seems to be a common theme in many of the letters I have read from emigrants writing home to Tyrone. As for John Dunlap, he printed 200 copies of the American Declaration of Independence and only 25 remain. All are considered priceless, but recently a copy turned up attached to the back of a picture that a man purchased for a few dollars in a flea market. I'm sure if John Dunlap is looking down from above on the banks of the Mourne he'll be well pleased for currently this copy is estimated to be worth $8 million.

One interesting thing I discovered from records of early times was that before the Ordnance Survey of Ireland (pub-

The River Mourne

lished in 1846) distances were recorded in Irish miles, and an Irish mile was a big mile – almost a third longer than the standard mile. As I said earlier, one of my predecessors covering these miles was Dr John Gamble. Riding into Strabane on horseback in the early 1800s he thought the vista was beautiful. Though mind you he changed his opinion when he got closer, having found *'squalid wretchedness',* in some parts of the town. John Gamble grew up in Strabane and was a military surgeon before he took to touring Ireland and writing books. It's from Gamble that we learn about Strabane's lying clock that could never tell the correct time. And he gives us an insight into a meal of the day at a local farm – '*…mutton, lamb and tongue, followed by candied gooseberries and a rich pudding washed down with a tolerable port and immense jugs of whiskey punch*'. I must say I got no such fare on my journey but no wonder that Dr John Gamble showed such good will towards Strabane.

Shortly after Gamble, Samuel Lewis compiled what he called his *Topographical Dictionary for Ireland,* using Taylor and Skinner's maps of the late 1700s, Cootes Survey 1801, Pigott's Directory of Ireland 1824 and other sources such as educational returns and the 1831 census of Ireland. Writing in 1837 Lewis complained of the difficulties he had with his compilation – mind you it's not hard to believe when you think about the span of time it drew from. And it's no surprise that the outcome for Tyrone was a bit like the flow of some of its rivers – a meandering mixture of history, folklore, agricultural and geological statistics – and some of it of questionable accuracy. That said, we learn that the Strabane area was dry and fertile, with orchards in abundance. Linen was often brought in its rough brown unbleached state to the markets and in the surrounding countryside there were few sheep but plenty of pigs. Lewis records that the numbers living in Strabane were about 6000 – here he must have meant Strabane and district for the 1841 census records a headcount of 4,704. And these days as an indication of just how much the town has grown the most recent census shows something of the order of 15000 people living in Strabane

For a final few insights into Strabane and the River Mourne I turn to the excellent volume *The Fair Valley River* edited by John Dooher and Michael Kennedy. Herein amongst the many names of people who had gone on to make fame for themselves in one way, or another, I discover the mathematical genius William Starrat, who excelled with breath taking brilliance in the skills of surveying and mapping; then there's man of letters Dr George Sigerson – James Joyce was one of his students. Another interesting character was William Collins who, as a boy, having crossed the Mourne, met a pedlar at nearby Castlefinn and as a result decided to devote himself to poetry. Collins spent most of his life in America and it was his nostalgic reflections on the far side

Strabane

The Town of Strabane

43

The River Mourne

of the world that produced lines perhaps not heard so much these days but often quoted years ago:

Oh God be with the good times when I was twenty-one
In Tyrone among the bushes where the Finn and Mourne run.

Also in the Strabane book, the late Jim Bradley reminds us that the writer Brian O' Nolan, otherwise Flann O'Brien, loved to lie in the long grass with his brothers on cloudless, dreamy summer days, watching the River Mourne and listening to the hum of the turbines coming from Sion Mills. O'Nolan went on to write one of the masterpieces of the twentieth century – *At Swim Two Birds* – and despite difficult times in his life always remembered the river with fondness.

Yet, as I said at the beginning, rivers can have moods and after unbelievable rains in the autumn of 1987 the River Mourne displayed the tempestuous side of its nature by flooding the entire centre of Strabane. A water wall had been in place since the 1800s to protect against such an event but it gave way and the result was utter devastation. The good that came out of it was unbelievable community spirit and neighbourliness and stout new concrete walls that run along both banks of the river through the centre of the town. And while it's a rather plain channel of water now it in no way lessens the attractiveness of the Strabane viewed from the bridge on the new bypass. There are two roundabouts here – one provides a route to Lifford in County Donegal, while near the other you find the striking sculpture Let the Dance Begin. This comprises five figures, each about 20 feet high and made of stainless steel strips in the distinct anatomical style of artist Maurice Harron. Two of the figures are dancers and three are musicians and they have been christened The Tinneys by the locals – probably because of their eerie metallic presence.

From here it's only a short distance across the bridge into the town of Lifford in County Donegal. The road follows the direction of the River Mourne, which now bears slightly to the left – the remaining few yards crossing fairly ordinary terrain in an uneventful way. Then suddenly – and indeed it is without warning, you find another waterway presenting itself. Flowing in from west Donegal is the River Finn. It has neither the power nor the width of the Mourne and looks somewhat darker in colour. Yet these two streams that have been roughly parallel with one another for some miles are now destined to come together. It's a meeting of the waters that gives them both equal status for they join each other at about the same angle. The rounded piece of land opposite where the confluence takes place is a well-known local spot called The Point. After this we have a new river and a mighty one at that – one that gives its name to the whole system, and one that through its association with Derry is much famed in history – the River Foyle.

A part of the journey has finished for me – I am saying goodbye to the River Mourne and greeting the River Finn. The Mourne strikes me as a truly energetic river always racing along – acclaimed for its beauty from its beginnings near Newtownstewart and famed for its salmon fishing. And here truly is a river that has relationships with people in a big way. There are the hymns and poems of Cecil Francis Alexander – and then the huge flax-spinning operation at Sion Mills that drew in thousands of folk over the generations. What a partnership between river and community that was, with stories of adventure, progress, love, triumph and no doubt sadness as well. And then Strabane – the settlement at the bend on the river that allowed people to exercise their talents near and far.

Certainly the River Mourne is very different from the streams in the upper reaches of the system – but then I realise that as a river it couldn't be what it is without the contributions of those self-same streams. I shall try to hold of all of this in mind in my travels along the River Finn.

To prepare for this next part of the journey it's first necessary to travel to the head waters of the Finn. This entails a trip by car to Lough Finn, where the river rises in Donegal's Blue Stack Mountains. As the saying goes it will take another dawn and another day and what better way to say farewell to the Mourne than with some lines from one of the poems by Cecil Frances Alexander:

The Mourne, like glittering serpent, roll'd his length
O'er his rough bed around Strabane's white wall,
And gently, like a bride, the silver Finn
Came through her meadows, wandering to meet
His bounding wave by Lifford's silent tower.
And it was beautiful to trace their course…

The River Finn

The River Finn - the Beginning

The River Finn to Ballybofey and Stranorlar

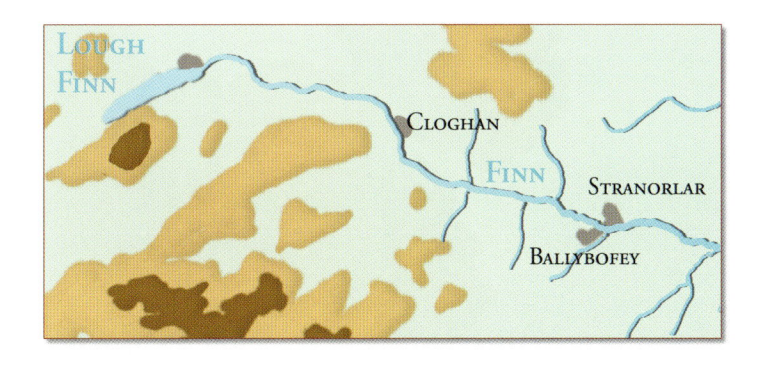

The River Finn runs eastwards out of Lough Finn through a valley in the Bluestack Mountains which eventually takes it to the twin towns of Ballybofey and Stranorlar. The same route is taken by the R252 road from the town of Glenties in west Donegal, and a second road from Glenties the R253 joins up with the R252 at Glenmore Bridge, Welchtown, just about a mile from Ballybofey.

Having arrived at Lough Finn in the highlands of Donegal, I'm feeling quite pleased with myself for without any great amount of searching I've found the source of the River Finn. It flows directly out of the east end of the lough and under the little bridge on which I'm standing. There's no show and no drama – in fact, I have to look twice to make sure that this is the beginning of one of the legendary rivers in the Foyle system.

The River Finn

I've often heard how some great waterways start as nothing more than a trickle on a mountainside and I can tell you the River Finn is not all that different. Barely a dozen feet wide and about a foot deep it slips silently and unobtrusively away into the nearby bog – its colour a rather pale brown. And really the contrast with the larger, free-flowing River Strule, about sixty odd miles to the east as the crow flies, could not be greater. Also different is the nature of the terrain – for while the Strule winds its way through rich farmland, here there are only barren peaks as far as the eye can see. These are the Bluestack Mountains (Na Cruacha Gorma – the Blue Mountains), or the Croaghs, as they're called locally. Lying in south Donegal they virtually divide the county in two and are themselves split near their lower end by Barnesmore Gap, the famous scenic route. In this landscape you are frequently confronted with massive shoulders of stark, grey granite, sitting out against the skyline. You see sharp rocky ridges and summits with tough sinewy heather and gorse – there are steep green braes, sheer drops, and hidden streams and lakes with crystal clear water. Everything here is elemental and well caught in the words of Ulster writer Louis McNeice:

> 'Both bountiful and callous, harsh and wheedling-
> In the constituencies of quartz and bog-oak…
> Here add one stone to the indifferent cairn…'

It's wild, rugged and stunning country – a hill walkers' paradise – in fact there's a trail through the mountains called the Bluestack Way. Yet care should be exercised in this range – it has all the appeal of a terrible beauty but in bad weather it's unforgiving and at times can be downright dangerous.

This then is where the River Finn first sees the light of day. Lough Finn from which it flows nestles in a steep-sided valley. It's deep and pencil-thin, being about 3 miles long and less than half a mile wide. Croaghleheen Mountain dominates on the left as does Aghla and Scraigs (Rocky Place) on the right. On the lower slopes of Aghla Mountain the deep green woods are particularly pleasing to the eye and there are narrow stretches of tough grassy moorland around the lough itself, which is 550 feet above sea level.

This is Gaeltacht country, where Irish is spoken, and part of the challenge for me is to unravel some of the meanings of the Gaelic words for place names. You may remember back at the River Strule I mentioned John O'Donovan's historical field work and the drive to anglicise Irish place names in the Ordnance Survey of the 1830s. One Gaelic speaker from the Finn Valley told me he thought the meaning of the original Irish had suffered badly in the translations – something not far from the theme of Brian Friel's play of the same name. And it brought me to thinking about the relationships people have with the land in places like the

Lough Finn

The Finn - Gathering Strength

49

The River Finn

Bluestacks. One of the interesting features of the early Irish language was the way it identified with particular locations, and it seems to me that the folk of those times had an altogether different, perhaps more intimate relationship, with things around them, than we have in today's world. I discovered that on the slopes of Aghla alone there used to be as many as twenty different Irish names for places that locals identified with. Another thing I notice here is that apart from using 'Crogh' to name mountains like Croaghleheen, the word 'Min', or 'Meen' is often used where there is a stretch of level ground, perhaps a smooth slope, or a flat top, for example Meenagolan. The contrast with the Sperrin Mountains, where Mullagh is used so much for rounded summits is interesting.

Now are the Bluestacks blue? Certainly on this day at the start of the journey and now in February there's not the slightest hint of blue. Fairly persistent rain has dragged a filmy grey mist down onto the lower slopes above Lough Finn and to be honest the mountains and surrounding countryside are devoid of colour. But I know this area well – I've seen it in all seasons and I've certainly witnessed the blue of the Bluestacks. Talking to local folk I find various views about the colour. Some feel the blue occurs as a result of light hitting the rock of the Croaghs, which is mainly granite composed of mica, quartz and feldspar. Others feel it's because of the flora in these parts, and others still, that the nature of the surrounding moist atmosphere allows a blue colour to predominate. Certainly the hue varies both with the hour of day, the conditions, and the time of the year. Though I must say on most occasions I've found it to be a misty light blue colour. I've read where the Blue Ridge Mountains of Virginia owe their colour – a blue haze – to the pine trees in the region, while for the Blue Mountains of Australia it's all down to the Eucalyptus forests. In the Nilgiri Hills of India near the famous hill station of Ootacmund (Ooty), an exquisite sapphire blue mist is said to float between the peaks – again, apparently it's down to the forests and the local flora. My encyclopaedia lists seventy shades of blue. So, since it's a colour much related to emotions perhaps without further ado it's best to allow travellers to make up their own minds about this mysterious hue that appears majestically at times over the mountains above the River Finn.

From Lough Finn the river has a 40 mile journey to make before it meets the River Mourne near Lifford. On this stretch I am following the Finn to Ballybofey and Stranorlar along its banks, but also taking the R252 where this gives me good views of the surrounding landscape. The journey will require several visits to the Finn Valley for approaches to the river banks can be demanding and time consuming in places. Also, the promise of an early spring – of which I entertained some hopes while travelling the Strule and the

Mourne – has turned out to be a nothing but a 'false spring'. Therefore I shall have to go as the elements permit.

By the way, the name of the lough and the river comes from a colourful but sad tale. In ancient times a beautiful young maid with long flaxen hair called Finngheal (or Finne – Fair One) heard her brother cry out for assistance as he was attacked nearby. She swam across the lake to help him, sword in hand and with her hair tied up. But because of the echo of the young man's cries she became confused as to his whereabouts. Then her hair fell down and in the entanglement of her tresses tragically she was drowned. From that time Finn became the name of the lough and also the river flowing out of it – and sometimes you find the River Finn referred to as the 'Fair One'.

Just where the river leaves Lough Finn at its eastern end you find the little community of Fintown. It's quiet now but saw busier times when trains came through here several decades ago. Fintown was a stop on the rail link from the town of Stranorlar to Glenties. It was part of the amazing network of narrow gauge railways established in the late 1800s that covered most of Donegal and ceased to operate in 1959. I expect I shall find evidence of embankments, arches and crossings as I go, for the Finn Valley Railway, which partially opened in 1863, followed the course of the river faithfully. That said, all is not lost with the railway for since the early 1990s a dedicated group of enthusiasts has laid a new 3-mile narrow gauge track along the path of the old railway beside Lough Finn. Short it may be but this small section of track is the only operational railway in County Donegal and a highly popular attraction close to where the River Finn rises.

However, I find that the Finn is practically lost from sight as it wanders off into the bog after leaving Lough Finn. Affairs are not helped by an abundance of rushes along the river banks but a little wood on the left relieves this rather plain stretch. Next I venture eastwards along the R252 road from where I see the Finn enter the tiny Lough Shivnagh (Rushy Place). Upon leaving here it collects several streams and burns from both sides of the valley and for awhile has a tendency to meander under Bellanamore Hill on the left bank. Opposite you see attractive, well wooded slopes flanking the Glashagh River and after this the Finn heads into a narrow gully and visibly begins to drop down through countryside. From here onwards the river is stronger and more assertive. It now has the familiar rich brown turf colour so typical of Ireland's bogland streams and the bed is absolutely littered with rocks. The effect of these rocks is quite amazing for as the river rushes past them it creates long white foamy trails just like tresses and my thoughts turn again to the legend of the girl Finngheal and how the river got its name.

The River Finn

The Salmon Leap

After a trek of some 3 miles and with conditions along the riverside not easy I come upon two delightful mountain streams - the Cummirk and the Elatagh – one on each side of Letterbrick (Breac'c Hill) and flowing into the Finn by way of the right bank. Actually, my map lists them as rivers but they're little more than wide burns. Their attractiveness to me is in the way they tumble down from the hills – enriched from the earth they travel in. Through bogs covered in heather, gorse and rushes they come – boisterous and impish, with an almost musical flow. All of which serves to swell the Finn and speed it up even more. One thing I realise now is that the River Finn is vastly different in character from the Strule and the Mourne. Wild, dark and broody on its journey through the mountains, it appears to pause occasionally in pools, making great whirls of foam, before dashing off once again along its boulder strewn course.

The stretch of the Finn Valley that lies roughly between Bellanamore Hill and Corraine near the town of Ballybofey – about 8 miles by road – is known as Glenfinn. It's along here that the River Finn has found fame as a great salmon river – much of it centred on Cloghan (The Stones). Actually, I find that some walking has to be done to get at the bank here since I'd approached by car along the R252 road that runs along the lower slopes of the hills above and back from the river. That said, the effort is really rewarding. After a little hairpin bend the Finn meets the River Reelan coming in on its right bank. This is a fascinating little mountain river, swift and foamy – it collects many streams from right in the heart of the Bluestacks. During my visit the weather brightens and with the water low I find some picturesque tranquil stretches near Reelan Bridge about a mile up stream from where this river meets the Finn. The bridge, which is famous in song, is a sturdy construction, with 3 arches. It must have looked impressive when it was built in the 1800s but rendering since then has taken away all the natural beauty of the stonework.

As for the River Finn at Cloghan, after collecting the Reelan it swings to the right to reveal a breathtaking scene. A series of pock-marked rocky beds fall off dramatically in steps over this stretch, which appears quite intriguing, almost secretive, to me. Both banks are tree-lined; there are dark pools and waterfalls large and small; and this spot has become renowned for its spectular Salmon Leap. The fish have to leap the natural steps – all of a sixty yard stretch – as they battle their way up river. It's a fascinating sight with the early run of salmon in the spring for the Finn is the earliest river in the whole of the Foyle system. It should be added that salmon fishing is prohibited in this unique part of the river – often referred to as the Sanctuary.

Yet the spot that intrigues me most is the pool at the nearby Ivy Bridge (Cloghan Bridge). This place is rocky, overgrown

The River Finn

and claustrophobic. Looking down from the bridge I get sense of a presence that's difficult to explain. For me there's an atmosphere here – something in the air – a definite feeling of times past. It's a bit like that feeling you get inside an ancient building when you sense memories are stored in the stone. But whether it's some sort of imprint of things that have happened on these banks, or of people that have been here, I cannot tell. You see, this place has seen folk from before the Celts; it has witnessed the kinsmen of Columcille (St Columba), seen the Plantation, the famine and the great exodus of people to America and Britain – does it hold secrets I wonder? What tales lie untold?

Certainly the mention of Columcille reminds me of one strange yarn about this part of the River Finn that was given to Adamnan, the saint's biographer. Adamnan recalls that as a youth he met Ernan, later St Ernan, who with other monks had been fishing in the deep pools along the Finn on the night of 9 June 597 AD. According to Ernan suddenly the sky lit up. Then a pillar of fire appeared in the east and slowly moved into the heavens so that night turned to day across the whole of the Finn Valley, striking fear into everyone. It was only later they heard that St Columba had died that same instant on Iona.

Talking of strange lights, another story is told in Glenfinn of a glowing, or flickering light that may be seen in late evenings in the countryside around the River Finn. This strange occurrence is not much reported nowadays but has been described as moving about the land with a mind of its own. Some people put it down to the will-o'-the-wisp effect that may be seen in boggy areas, but others say the glow only occurred during extensive mining of iron ore in Glenfinn during World War II. Yet you still meet some hereabouts who feel the appearance of the moving light is a warning – a portent of sad news. One Irish folklore story about this strange glow involves a farmer who owes the Devil money but tricks him into climbing a tree to retrieve it. Once there the wily farmer puts a cross on the tree thus preventing the Devil from coming down. A deal is struck removing all obligations on the farmer, but when he dies the Devil won't have in him in hell and likewise St Peter bars him from Heaven. As a result, the farmer's spirit is doomed to wander the banks of the Finn and sometimes you get a sight of him at night for the Devil has given him a present – a glowing ember to light his way. I suppose there's no need to tell you it was lit from the fires of hell.

Incidentally, one son of Glenfinn, who would have roamed the banks of the Finn as a boy in the 1820s was Isaac Butt. His father was the local rector. Isaac Butt grew up to be a brilliant lawyer and politician. Initially, he was a Conservative, but later defended the Nationalist cause, advocating non-violence. After stirring times his political career some-

Cloghan

The Sanctuary, the Finn

The River Finn

what fizzled out and he had problems in his personal life. Eventually, he died at the age of 65. A modest man, never given to religious bigotry, Butt wrote, *'Put no inscription over my grave, except the date of my birth and the date of my death … let the funeral be perfectly private'.* But Glenfinn has not forgotten Isaac Butt, for his memory lives on in the Isaac Butt Heritage Centre based at the old Brockagh National School in Cloghan.

Back to the river at Cloghan and I come upon a residence I've often heard about – Cloghan Lodge. This half-timbered mock Tudor house in black and white was built in 1820 by General Sir Charles Styles. He'd distinguished himself in the wars of the early 1800s and in recognition of his services was given 60,000 acres of Glenfinn to develop as an estate for hunting and fishing – thus the lodge, which sits in its own 60 acres of land. It was landscaped in the 1830s with trees, shrubs and attractive paths and provides some very fascinating walks. Apart from the main dwelling and its outhouses, amongst the other interesting buildings here is the Broth House. Dating back to the days of the Famine (1847), you can still see the hole in the wall through which the broth was ladled to the queues of starving folk. The Styles family sold the property in 1920 and since then various arrangements have been in place with regard to fishing rights along this part of the River Finn – a further development has been the recent sale of Cloghan Lodge for a substantial sum of money.

Below Cloghan the course of the Finn straightens, giving a more rapid flow than at the Ivy Bridge. As I make my way down the right bank one of the features I like is the abundance of trees and shrubs – in the variations of light and shade they lend quite a mysterious feel to the whole setting of the river here. I've even noticed beech and rhododendron, which surely is another indication of the landscaping efforts in the early 1800s. My crossover point is at the stone footbridge, which allows me access to the opposite bank and the R250 road again. I assume this narrow little bridge, less than a mile below the Ivy Bridge, was originally built in the early 1900s to allow worshipers to cross to the newly built Roman Catholic chapel of Our Lady of Perpetual Succour, which is on the left bank.

About a mile further along the R252 I pause to view the Finn from Glenmore Bridge at Welchtown and estimate the depth to be about five feet, with the flow still brisk. Nearby is St John's Church (Church of Ireland) erected in 1879. Incidentally, Isaac Butt's father was a rector of the original church. And on the subject of faith, certainly it seems to me that religious practice has a long tradition in the valley of the Finn. This particular parish is ancient and has an unusual name – Kilteevogue, which is attributed to St Taovog,

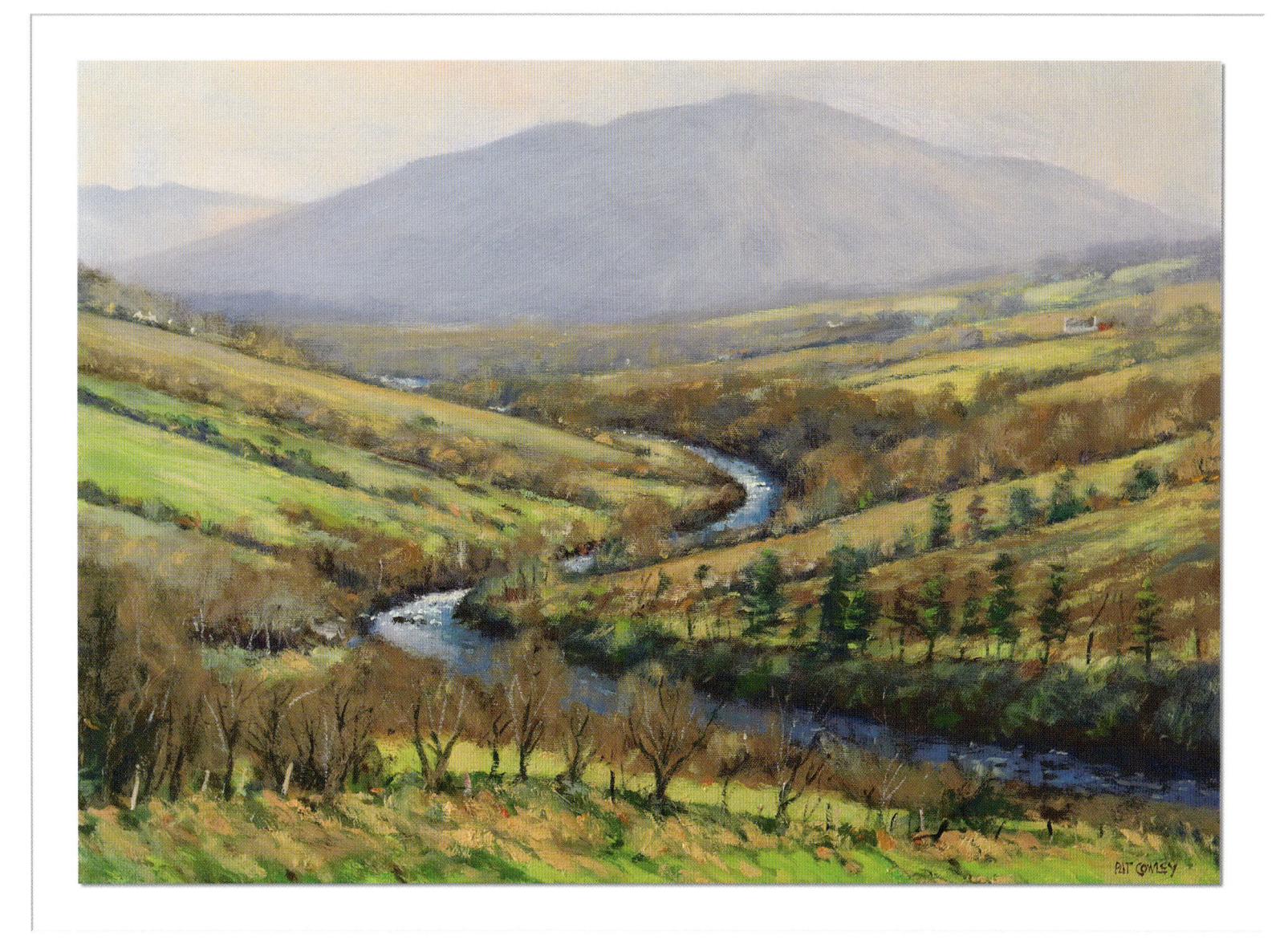

Glenfinn

Glenfinn

The River Finn

the daughter of a chieftain, who became a nun after her father was converted to Christianity by St Patrick.

Just at St John's Church the R252 meets the R253, which is another magnificent scenic route through the centre of the Bluestacks between Glenties and Ballybofey. And seeing the R253 jogs my memory about my first ever climb in the Bluestacks. A few years ago I set out with a group of friends to go in search of the wreckage of the World War II aeroplane that had crashed here in January 1944. I remember taking the R253 and skirting the conical, steep-sided Altnapaste mountain. Eventually, we arrived at a spot near McDevitt's Bridge on the Owenea River and found the path that would take us up into the mountains. We were headed for one of the Bluestacks' highest summits – our landmark being a large white quartz crystal rock not far from where the plane had crashed.

The going was tough and not helped by constant showers of rain that soon became a persistent downpour. The mountain gets steeper as you go – I remember it was the typical climb – just when you thought you'd conquered the final shoulder another lay waiting. None the less we found the plane. To be honest all that remained was pieces of wreckage strewn over the ground. The aircraft was a Mark III Sunderland Flying Boat that had been on a reconnaissance mission down the west coast of Ireland. It seems the crew's home base was in Wales but due to bad weather they'd been diverted to Castle Archdale on the shores of Lough Erne.

Somehow the Sunderland got off course, touched the crest of the mountain and crashed in a ball of fire. Seven of the crew were killed but five survived and local folk were much praised for their rescue efforts. On my climb I realised what an ordeal it must have been for those airmen in 1944, for the weather turned really bad on us and we had to beat a hasty retreat down the mountain. I recall clambering over treacherous rocks and then slipping and sliding down a steep grassy brae that swept away into the valley hundreds of feet below. Finally, we had to wade across a river that had been no more than a little stream when we started our climb.

Ours was a memorable trip but nothing compared to the heroics of Jim Gilchrist the last surviving member of that Sunderland crew. In April 2003 at the age of eighty, Jim returned to the crash site for a commemorative ceremony. He had raised the alarm back in 1944 by scrambling down the mountain, but on this occasion he returned to the scene in an Irish Air Corps helicopter. And once again he braved the absolutely treacherous conditions to lay a wreath of poppies at the scene where so many of his young colleagues had died. Sadly, Jim himself has now passed on.

Ballybofey and Stranorlar

By the way, the statistics of the Mark III Sunderland give you some idea of the catastrophe – it had a wingspan of 112 feet, a length of 85 feet and a height of 32 feet. Its weight was almost 30 tons and it was loaded with munitions and still had half its fuel. During the War the Sunderland plane was dreaded by the Germans, who christened it the 'Flying Porcupine' on account of the numerous gun positions jutting from the fuselage. For the record, the plane that crashed in the Bluestacks was one of 461 Mark IIIs made by Short and Harland in Belfast.

Back to the River Finn at Glenmore Bridge and here it bids goodbye to the Bluestacks. It now takes a somewhat winding course through much lower hills for about four miles to the town of Ballybofey. But you can't mention Ballybofey without also talking about Stranorlar. The pair are inevitably linked as the 'Twin Towns' and have been so since the 1800s. As for Ballybofey (Bealach Feich, or Baile bo Fiach), some say it means Fiach's Road, while others take it to be the portion of land that costs a cow in yearly tax. While for Stranorlar (Strath an Urlair), the meaning is more straightforward being the Flat Bottomed Valley. The River Finn separates the 'Twin Towns', with Ballybofey to the south and Stranorlar to the north.

I discovered that Stranorlar was first developed during the Plantation in about 1620 by Peter Benson who'd built the original walls of Derry between 1613 and 1618. In those days the River Finn acted as a sort of frontier post – a defence for the Planters living in Stranorlar against disaffected clans in Donegal. And while there was a ford here from ancient times it was the eventual building of a stone bridge over the river that brought the development of Ballybofey as we know it today – a friendly, thriving, commercial centre of at least 4000 people – leaving Stranorlar a much quieter spot.

Published in 1837, Lewis' *Topographical Dictionary* records that Stranorlar was a town and Ballybofey a village in the parish of Stranorlar. The main markets were in Stranorlar but since Ballybofey was on the coach route to Donegal town and Ballyshannon it had begun to expand as well. Stranorlar was also at the centre of the famous railway system that ran the complete length of the river and was called appropriately enough the Finn Valley Railway. As I noted back at Fintown it commenced in the 1860s. In time it became part of a 200-mile narrow gauge network usually known as the County Donegal Railways and affectionately called 'The Wee Donegal'. This railway, which wound up in 1959, played a major role in life of Donegal for nearly a hundred years and provided much employment.

Another source of jobs around the 'Twin Towns' in early times was the production of linen, especially from the 1700s

The River Finn

onwards. There were at least two local bleachgreens and one of these was in the vicinity of Summerhill – a residence, looking out over the Finn Valley from a rise above the town. The Johnsons of Summerhill had substantial control of the banks of the Finn on its passage eastwards out of Ballybofey towards Castlefin and the River Foyle. One of their major concerns was to keep the river water clean for bleaching purposes, so they applied very strict controls to where tanneries were located. Incidentally, linen manufacture in this part of Donegal was a cottage industry, where women would spin the flax fibres into thread and men would weave the fabric on small looms. Mostly brown linen was sold at Stranorlar market. This was rougher material, which would pass on to bleaching works elsewhere for refining. However, the linen industry throughout the north west would later decline as Belfast became a major centre for production.

As for the residence at Summerhill, according to Pigott's Directory (1824), the Johnsons were thoroughly settled there at that time, but later the property went to the Conynghams. People in Ballybofey tell me that many years ago they remembered seeing the last of the Conyngham family who lived there – two spinster ladies always dressed in black, who frequently rode into town in old fashioned bicycles from the big house. Now I've an interest in finding the Summerhill residence for there's a curiosity here the like of which you rarely see – a matrimonial tree.

Matrimonial Tree, Summerhill

And after climbing up out of Ballybofey I do find the house – but, what sadness. Summerhill is a total ruin, overgrown with ivy and trees – windows and doors are gone. The roof folds over in a curve through the first floor so that the big blue slates are splayed out in front of you like a pack of cards. There are stone outbuildings and several acres of land – obviously this was once a landscaped meadow but now is covered with decaying trees and bushes. Walking through this house, built about 1800, you are aware how it has gone the full circle as a dwelling – lovingly put together bit by bit by craftsmen, the reverse is happening now – walls have fallen; you find the plaster has come away from decorative ceilings to reveal a network of laths – in some places joists protrude through the floors, and on it goes until you come upon a room where the place is starkly open to the world and you see the sky above you. Indeed, the only sign there's been occupation here in times past is the square-shaped entrance hall that still has some of the original rouge red walls popular in houses of the time.

Suddenly through the frame of an empty window I see the curiosity I'm looking for in the garden at the back – the matrimonial tree – in fact there are a couple of sets of these trees. In all my travels around country houses I've never seen anything quite like this. Some families had the tradition in bygone times that when an engagement was announced two trees would be planted beside one another. When the wedding took place they would then be grafted and thereafter grow together. The result after many years would be two trees growing individually but joined at the splice in an arch that you can almost climb through. In keeping with the house, sadly, the matrimonial trees at Summerhill have collapsed with age. One set in the lower end of the garden consisting of two beeches has just the arch remaining – both trunks lie broken to the side. The other set, which is of oak, is completely torn apart at the arch, with just one of the trees still standing. I suppose in a way it's a reminder of human mortality. These trees appear to be more than 150 years old – they look desolate and abandoned now. I ponder on what tales might be told, but it looks as if we shall never know the stories of the sweethearts who strolled in this strange and melancholy garden on the hill above the River Finn. As I turned for a last glance at Summerhill the words of a Longfellow poem came to me:

> *'All houses wherein men have lived and died*
> *Are haunted houses. Through the open doors*
> *The harmless phantoms on their errands glide,*
> *With feet that make no sound upon the floor*
> *And from the world of spirits there descends*
> *A bridge of light, connecting it with this…'*

The River Finn

The Finn below the 'Twin Towns'

62

The Finn to the Foyle

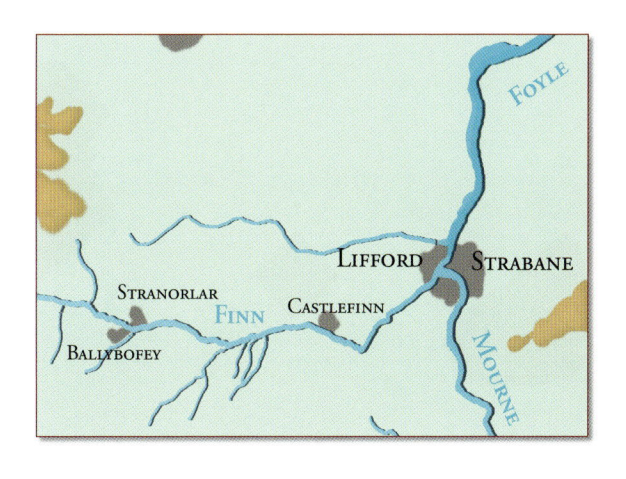

The River Finn now takes a lazy, meandering course eastwards through the Finn Valley to the village of Killygordon and on to the town of Castlefinn. It then turns to the northeast passing Clady and Urney, where it shares its right bank with Northern Ireland. From Urney it takes a straight run into the confluence with the River Mourne between Lifford and Strabane. The N15 road runs all the way alongside the Finn and at Lifford meets the N14 coming from Letterkenny.

There are many who would refer to this stretch of the river between the 'Twin Towns' of Ballybofey and Stranorlar and Lifford as the Finn Valley proper – as distinct from the valley of the Finn, which would be the whole of the river. So, it's along the Finn Valley that I now trek in the direction of the town of Castlefinn. From the 'Twin Towns' the River Finn keeps a straight course and still flows strongly for the next mile or so. If you could look back more than a hundred years you'd see the waterwheels and the millraces that helped

The Finn to the Foyle

drive the scutch and corn mills all along the banks here. In June the whole countryside would take on an intense blue hue from the countless acres of flax flowers but afterwards the preparation of the flax itself in the so called 'lint' dams left the most awful smell everywhere.

Just where the river swings left here is known as Edenmore and I couldn't move on without recounting a fishing tale associated with this stretch. Local fishermen say that best colours for flies on the Finn are red, orange, yellow and gold. But, apparently back in the early 1920s something quite different created a big stir. Over a cup of tea in Ballybofey a lady told me how her grandfather, having run out of bait, clipped off a little bit of his beard, tied it to a hook, and commenced to fly-fish with it. There was nothing for a while until an almost casual cast brought a flash of silver and a splash that was nearly heard back in the town – or so I was told. Anyway, that unusual catch turned out to be a monster salmon at over 33lbs in weight. It must have been great fishing back in those days for in 1922 a woman fishing on the River Tay in Scotland hooked what is still a record for a salmon on rod and line at a staggering 64 lbs.

Now on my journey, I notice that the River Finn starts to meander – a little at first and then quite significantly. It's almost as if it were becoming lazy. Certainly it's slower and deeper now as the valley flattens out and in a way is strangely quiet – I recall that quote from the Roman poet Horace – *'The deepest rivers flow with the least sound'* – and you know there's truth in it.

As regards the landscape, in contrast to the Bluestacks the surrounding hills are quite small and roll away pleasantly towards the horizon. Occasionally you see evidence of the old Finn Valley Railway on the left bank and soon the little village of Killygordon comes into sight. At this stage I'm about halfway between the 'Twin Towns' and Castlefin. Along with its 7-arch bridge built in 1782, Killygordon now boasts a recently constructed metal footbridge. On the right bank nearby is the little village of Crossroads, where I was most impressed by the steeple of St Patrick's Church. On the left bank of the river a secondary road takes you the short distance northwards to Raphoe, a place immersed in history since the Stone Age.

The town of Raphoe (Rath Bhoth – The Fort of the Huts) is in the centre of a fertile plain which extends to Lough Swilly in the north west of Donegal. Generally referred to as the Laggan (Low Level Countryside) it was known to the ancient peoples as the Plain of Magh Itha and saw many tribal battles. By the mid-1800s there were 1400 people living in Raphoe and today that figure has fallen to 1000. The Laggan was a favourite location for Planters in the 17th century and you can see that in the triangular shape of Ra-

Raphoe

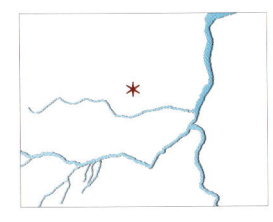

Beltany Stone Circle,
Raphoe

65

The Finn to the Foyle

phoe's Diamond, which very much reflects the Plantation style. The many old buildings hereabouts give an antique feel to the entire neighbourhood and the area has always had strong Church connections. It is thought that St Patrick may have been an early visitor. Later in the middle of the sixth century St Columba founded a monastery at this site and Adamnan (St Eunan) his biographer was born here. There is a story that Columba restored the life of a drowned man at Raphoe and gave a boy a blessing that made him into an expert blacksmith.

These days Raphoe has a Catholic bishop and it had a Protestant bishop until 1833, when the diocese became Derry and Raphoe. Yet long before the early Church in Raphoe pre-Christain worship was practised here. On a hill about a mile outside the town you come upon archaeological remains that are frequently referred to as Ireland's Stonehenge. Beltany Stone Circle is regarded as one of the finest stone circles in Ireland. It contains 64 standing stones out of an original 80 – the heights range from 4 feet to 9 feet, the diameter is 145 feet, and the date is put at well before 2000 BC. There is a suggestion that the sun god Baal (or perhaps the Celtic god Belenus) was worshipped here. It seems that fires were lit on the first day of May – the Celtic festival of Bealtine – thus the name Beltany. I've visited quite a few stone circles on my travels and found all of them fascinating. But Beltany impresses me most since it's on a rise and from a lower level you can see it quite dramatically against the skyline. Does it have a mystical feel, or a presence? I think you'd have to visit on the summer or winter solstices, or perhaps the spring or autumn equinoxes, to grapple with that question. Without putting too much of a damper on it the most recent explanation of the strange stones is that they are sort of ancient calendar whose alignments helped the Neothlithic peoples mark significant periods of the year.

Dropping back southwards from Raphoe I take the secondary road that after four miles will bring me to the River Finn at Castlefinn. I go by this route because it allows me to view the River Deele that eventually flows into the Foyle just below Lifford – in fact it is the first waterway that the River Foyle collects in its own right. If ever there was a wanderer it is the River Deele. Rising in the eastern end of the Bluestacks in Lough Deele it twists and turns all the way across the lower Laggan Valley – a distance of 37 miles. It is a small river and with all its meandering I find it to be very sluggish. And though it lies not much more than a couple of miles from the River Finn the two are never destined to meet, separated as they are by the low range of hills that guard the left side of Finn Valley.

Castlefinn itself is a neat little town of about a 1000 people. My map shows it to be at a sort of hub between the 'Twin Towns' and Lifford running west to east and between Ra-

Castlefinn and Clady

phoe and Castlederg running north to south. It's said that the stones from an O'Donnell castle – from which the town gets its name (Caislean na Finne) – went into the building of the bridge that now carries the R235 road in the direction of Castlederg. Like many other places my feeling is that Castlefinn saw more life in the days of the railway – people going to both Donegal and Glenties from Derry, or Strabane, would have travelled through here. I counted seven daily return journeys from early morning to late evening on an old railway timetable that I came across. And though you mightn't think it now, boats carrying a burden of 14 tons came up to Castlefinn from Derry. In fact, this is how the railway tracks were brought in to build the Finn Valley Railway.

Just 2 miles further down stream I come upon the village of Clady. What strikes me about the ground I have covered from Castlefinn is that the land around the banks is flat and the river has commenced to twist and turn again. It also seems to me that the Finn is tidal along this stretch, so there must be times when nature conspires to cause quite a lot of flooding in this area. Another interesting feature is that the River Finn has entered Tyrone – at least on its right bank – the boundary with the Republic of Ireland now more or less runs through the centre of the river.

By the way, I take Clady to derive from the Irish Claddagh – Muddy Bank of the River, since this fits in with the tidal conditions. But there are other suggestions about the origin of the name. It's something you can reflect on as you look down from the 7-arch stone bridge that takes folk from Clady over to the Republic of Ireland. There's only room for single file traffic here and tiny recesses allow those on foot to avoid oncoming vehicles. With the Republic so near it's no surprise to hear that there are legendary tales of smuggling going back over the decades.

There was a well-known ford here in times past and this brings to mind another episode. A famous encounter took place at Clady when the troops of James II overcame the defenders of Derry prior to the Siege. History books talk of the battle at Clady Ford on 15 April 1689 and sometimes there is the impression that James' men crossed the ford that day. However, that was not strictly the case because the river was in flood and the ford unusable. What appears to have happened is that the troops managed to cross a broken wooden bridge with the aid of planks, while others swam across the Finn holding on to their horses. The Derry defenders retreated to fight another day and James later arrived at this spot when the clamour had died down. Apparently he needed a rest from his journey up through Ireland and there is a tradition that he dined under a sycamore tree in the garden of Cavanacor House near Lifford. Another story tells

The Finn to the Foyle

of James smitten with a cold in the desperately wet weather and having fits of sneezing – thus the nick-name Sneezing Hill for one of the nearby slopes. By the way, because of his friendly welcome at Cavanacor James later spared the house upon his retreat from Derry.

Underway again and my map indicates that I am now about 4 miles from where the River Finn joins the River Mourne. As I move northwards along the Finn towards this confluence, nearby, Strabane lies to the right and Lifford to the left. Downstream next door to Clady I reach the parish of Urney (Place of Prayer). The river continues to be listless here and the valley still very flat. This looks very much to be arable land now but I've no doubt that flax was grown here when the linen industry was flourishing. I also get the feeling that Urney has been lived in for a very long time. There has always been a strong religious tradition in this community and today all denominations are well represented in the churches hereabouts. Indeed, I learn that Urney had a very early religious settlement – St Safan, a nun of great wisdom, was linked to a monastery here in the 8th century.

Thinking about those far off times it's my belief that there was an ancient path running from Urney over to the River Mourne barely 3 miles east of here. And that brings me to October 1397 and Archbishop Colton's bid to take on the might of Derry – he would have taken this old path. You'll recall on our journey down the Mourne that we pictured Colton's party setting out from Ardstraw on the way to Urney. After travelling downstream they would have turned left just about where Sion Mills village is today and headed west towards the River Finn and their destination. Messengers had been sent on ahead and a group of Urney church folk was there to welcome the travellers. Again they got the same warm reception as at Ardstraw and guards were placed outside their lodgings overnight. Yet despite the mounting danger Colton was anxious to get underway the following morning. He planned to stop at Leckpatrick, a little community about 4 miles north of Strabane. Here he wanted to change horses for the final approach to Derry. But his diarist reveals that this particular sojourn at Leckpatrick had nothing like the civility of previous stopovers. Perhaps cold rather than hostile, it was the first real sour note on the journey. No doubt Colton would have wondered was it a sign of things to come for by dusk he would be insight of Columcille's Derry. We shall see how he fared when I meet the main River Foyle a little later on the journey.

Now you may recall that I talked about the Newtownstewart murders when I was travelling along the River Strule. Just before leaving Urney there's yet another spine-chilling fact to relate. The notorious William Burke, yes he of the murderous partnership of Burke and Hare, came from Urney. Burke married and for a while was with the Donegal

Urney

Militia before he abandoned his family and went to Scotland. In time he was found guilty of some thirty murders – corpses for Edinburgh doctors – and was hanged in the city in December 1828. His skeleton can still be viewed in Surgeon's Hall in Edinburgh. And there is something else for us to remember Burke by. When Hare asked his accomplice if their murderous spree was not getting out of hand, the Urney man retorted with the famous words that have long outlived him – *"Sure we might as well be hanged for a sheep as a lamb!"*

As I leave Urney I find myself wondering did Burke go down stream from here and sail from Derry Quay? That's all conjecture of course and here in the reality of my trek I find the last couple of miles of the Finn below Urney to be uneventful. The flow quickens a little as the river runs a more direct course and the ground is noticeably flat and wider on the approach to the confluence with the Mourne. Just where the rivers come together the waterway swings to the left and directly opposite on the right bank of the Mourne is The Point – the promontory I talked about earlier. From here onwards to the ocean is the great river that gives its name to the whole system – the Foyle.

About fifty yards away you can see the bridge from Strabane into Lifford – built in 1964 it replaced the famous Lifford Bridge, which from 1730 saw much coming and going to Donegal – local people, emigrants, traders, travellers, visitors, the great and the good, all used this well-known crossing. And apart from serving as a frontier between Northern Ireland and the Republic from the 1920s the centre of this bridge was always taken as the county boundary between Tyrone and Donegal. This led to an unusual tradition during the 1800s. It appears that juries not able reach a decision in the local courts could only be dismissed at the county boundary. Since this was at the centre of Lifford Bridge the poor jury folk were paraded on the celebrated old bridge before being released from their duties – by all accounts it was a very odd spectacle indeed.

Of course Lifford Bridge is long gone but the meeting of the waters between Strabane and Lifford lives on. And naturally enough the coming together of the Mourne and the Finn is a real highlight on my journey. And that's not just because I'm saying goodbye to two remarkable waterways that I've got to know during my travels. You see I'm also witnessing the beginning of one of the finest rivers in Europe – the River Foyle.

But before I travel the banks of the Foyle to the sea some 28 miles away it's time for a final reflection on my journey along the Finn. When you think about it the River Finn is well and truly ruled by its landscape. Tumbling out of the wild and magnificent Bluestacks we see the river and raw

The Finn to the Foyle

nature together – apart from trying to eke out an existence, or the sport of fishing, perhaps the only other thing people can do is to admire it, or maybe celebrate it in one way, or another. I am reminded of writer Frank O' Connor's words as he journeyed through Ireland on his bicycle – *'Nature is all very well but it produces a ravenous appetite for civilisation…'* Having trekked through the vast emptiness of the magnificent Bluestacks I understand that.

Thinking about the lower reaches of the Finn it also seems to me that there are times, or perhaps I should say places, where the relationships between people and the river become thoroughly interdependent. For the Finn this happened when folk began to manage the waterway through mills, bleaching works, agriculture, markets and commerce. And building on that achievement the communities along the river are successful today. All of which tells me it's no accident that folk settle near rivers and choose locations where rivers can be harnessed and put to work in one way or other.

Finally, there's no doubting the imprints left behind in the relationship between people and rivers. It seems to me as if an ever changing destiny is at work. Sometimes the outcome is happy and sometimes it's sad. All along the banks of the River Finn you see evidence of this - perhaps it's a record salmon caught, or the bustle of the 'Twin Towns', or the sad emptiness of a broken down mill, or the desolation of an old house like Summerhill, where the roof has fallen in.

Whatever has happened, whatever the tales to be told, people have come and gone and the river rolls on.

The River Mourne

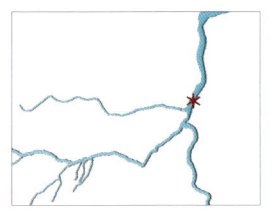

The Big Island, below Strabane

The River Foyle from Lifford to Derry City

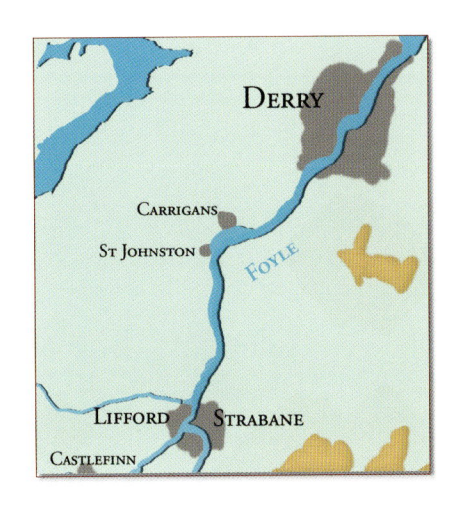

The River Foyle begins at the Mourne-Strule confluence and immediately meets the town of Lifford from where it has a straight run past the little community of Port Hall and on to the village of St Johnston. From here it swings slightly left and passes the village of Carrigans before taking a direct run into Derry City and on to Lough Foyle. The border with County Donegal in the Republic of Ireland runs through the centre of the river to a point 3 miles from Derry. From Strabane on the Northern Ireland side the A5 road follows the course of the river all the way to Derry – a distance of 12 miles. From Lifford, a secondary road at the Rossgeir turn-off follows the Foyle's left bank all the way to Derry.

Lifford is the first town you meet on the main River Foyle. It is located on the river's left bank. Now although there are records of river traffic in the 1700s, you get the impression that Lifford never used the waterway for commerce in any major way after the introduction of the Strabane Canal

The River Foyle

in 1792. Items would mainly have gone from Strabane to Lifford and vice versa by way of the bridge over the river. Having said that, Lifford is a fine market town with a population of about 2000 people but, like Strabane, it has been subject to the fluctuations of the modern economy. Lifford is a gateway both to the 'Twin Towns' of Ballybofey and Stranorlar and to Letterkenny. And while it's in no way a key economic centre, the town is the county seat for Donegal – a mark of its importance in past times. There was a monastic settlement in this neighbourhood in the 6th century but Lifford owes its origins to Manus O'Donnell, a Donegal chieftain, who built a castle here in 1526. Later, during the Plantation, a ferry was established across the Foyle and an English garrison was put in place, which remained until the formation of the Irish Free State in 1922.

Crossing the bridge from the Strabane direction a right turn takes you down into the older part of Lifford. There are narrow terrace streets here and there's a distinct feeling of times past. Eventually, you come upon a square containing Lifford Old Courthouse – this was also once the site of Lifford Jail. Built in 1746, the jail housed some notable prisoners in its day, among them John McNaughten, who killed his young sweetheart Mary Ann Knox. He lives on in Irish folklore as Half-hanged McNaughten, being so-called since the rope broke during the first attempt to hang him on the gallows. Later, in May 1878, Michael Heraghty and the McGranagahan brothers, Bernard and Thomas, of Fanad in Donegal, were committed for trial for the murder of the Third Earl of Leitrim, a hated landlord. The incident caused a sensation throughout Ireland. Heraghty died during an outbreak of typhoid in the jail – mind you some whispered that he'd

Lifford Jail

Lifford

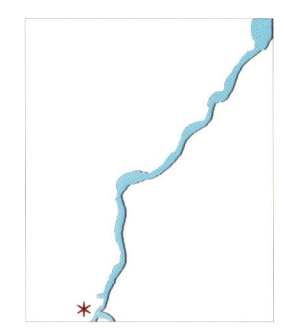

The Foyle Valley from Binnion Hill near Lifford

The River Foyle

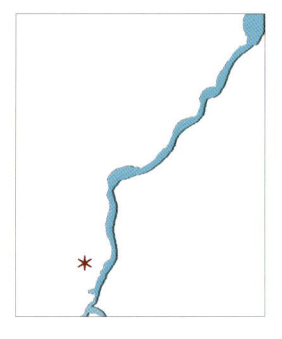

Looking across to Port Hall

Port Hall

been smuggled out to America. As for the McGranaghans, they were released the following February due to insufficient evidence and a party of 40 supporters cheered them on to the Strabane train for Derry, where they celebrated with a day's shopping.

Before leaving Lifford I also find that the Courthouse – now an excellent historical audio-visual centre – was designed in the 18th century by the Derry based architect Michael Priestley. It seems that Priestley was responsible for 4 of the great houses along the River Foyle. So I shall be on the outlook for his distinctive Georgian style and his unusual use of sandstone on the windows, doors and corners. This is known as Gibbsian rusticated stonework and comes from the pattern books of the Scottish architect James Gibbs.

As the River Foyle leaves Lifford the width across is about 80 feet and the depth at least 10 feet depending on the tide. From the left bank I see the remains of the stonework that supported the bridge taking the narrow gauge railway to Letterkenny. Incidentally, there were two railway bridges on the other side of Strabane – one for the Great Northern Railway and the other for the Finn Valley Railway, both these crossing the River Mourne. This gives you an idea just how busy a junction Strabane was in earlier times.

On with my journey, and it has now slipped into spring. There are some warm days, some showery ones and some windy. A distinct advantage is that there are more clear skies and that's a major blessing for this stretch of the Foyle is famed for the beauty of its landscape and I've hopes of seeing it at its best. One disadvantage is that it's not easy to trek along the river – it's difficult to get at the bank in places and once arrived there it's equally difficult to cover distances of any length. So this part of my expedition has had much more starting and stopping and going down lanes that sometimes lead to nowhere in particular, or leave me no nearer where I want to go. My solution is to target particular vantage points along the river and from these to explore as much of the surrounding countryside as possible.

The first destination is Port Hall just three miles from Lifford on the Foyle's left bank. I think the best approach is via the N14 road out of Lifford – you then take a right turn at Rossgeir to approach the river. On the way I come across the River Deele. It enters the Foyle here quietly and unnoticed, looking totally exhausted after its long and winding journey across the Laggan Valley. There are at least two houses of interest in Port Hall. Hall Green is said to date to 1611, which means it's been here since Plantation times. The house is attractively preserved having many of its early features and it was originally called Longvale House on account of the view across the Foyle valley. Nearby is Port Hall

The River Foyle

House, the first of the houses along the river attributed to the architect Michael Priestley. This tall and elegant dwelling is very much in the Priestley style but with an unusual semi-circular window set into the central pediment and while it's of the Georgian period it reflects very much the warm character of a big Irish country house.

A previous owner of Port Hall House was the colourful and talented Anthony (Tony) Marecco (d. 2006 aged 90). Tony Marecco was famous for his romantic liaisons with some of the most beautiful women of his day. He was married 4 times, having lastly remarried his second wife in 2004. The story goes that he may have purchased Port Hall by means of an inheritance from the famous Lali Horstmann, one of his lovers. Tony Marreco's good looks and charm were said to melt women's hearts – his assignations in the world of high society leave one breathless. This aside, he was in his time an actor, a barrister, a naval officer, and a British diplomat in Germany after World War II. Tony Marecco was a member of the British delegation at the Nuremberg trials and a founder member of Amnesty International. Always for justice and fair play, he took a great interest in all things Irish during his years in Ireland. This then was the intriguing man who loved to wander the banks of the River Foyle at Port Hall. He was said to be a magnificent raconteur and among the stories he could tell were of his meetings with Rudolf Hess and Hermann Goering at Nuremberg and as a youth his exchanges with Ghandi and Lawrence of Arabia back in the 1920s when they were guests at Westminister, his public school.

A laneway near Port Hall takes me towards the river via the former route of the Great Northern Railway (GNR) and I come upon an old bridge – Port Hall Bridge. This used to take the railway from Derry across to Corkan Island in the middle of river. From there another bridge carried it to the opposite bank and on to Strabane. This line ceased in 1965. However, the surface of the railway bridge has been covered to give access to the islands. You have to marvel at its solid construction – to manage such magnificent metal fabrication back in the middle of the 1800s in such a remote place is astounding although, of course, this is the same for all the railway bridges throughout the system. Technically there are 2 islands – Island More and Corkan. But they are only separated by a drain. I've also discovered that there was a ford at the top end of Island More where the sandy bed is shallow. In fact sand is very plentiful in the Foyle hereabouts and this most likely helped to establish Port Hall on the river bank.

As for the islands – surprisingly, they run a length of nearly 3 miles along the middle of the river before tailing off into a sand bank. Talking to people in the locality I learn a couple of interesting facts about these islands. The first concerns the border between Northern Ireland and the Republic of

Island More and Corkan Island

Ireland drawn up after 1922. As mentioned above it runs along the centre of the River Foyle. However, the islands in the river presented a dilemma since the new border would have run directly through them. Apparently the problem was solved in a novel way. The Border Commission decided that the River Foyle itself should provide the answer. So, they released a floating barrel from Lifford Bridge stating that whichever bank it touched would decide whether the islands would be in the North, or the Republic. The barrel drifted to the left bank and so the islands in the Foyle were declared to be in the Republic of Ireland.

The second story centres on hare coursing of which there's been a long tradition in the Lifford area. Hares are scarce in Ireland and it's said that when any were caught in times gone by they were kept on these islands and then dispatched to various parts of Ireland. Hare coursing is a very controversial subject and I am tempted to wonder could the poor things not have escaped by way of the railway bridges? Actually, the bridge taking the railway from Corkan Island to the Strabane side of the river was mostly taken away at the start of the 'Troubles' in the 1970s. I take the opportunity to see what's left of this crossing – known as McKinney's Bridge. All that remains now are 21 iron columns spaced out in sets of 3 across the width of the river. Yet it's a stunning spectacle – almost like a metal version the ancient Egyptian colonnades at Luxor.

Certainly you can see how the Foyle in these parts would have been much busier in past times and that's very evident straight across from Port Hall on the river's right bank. Here the Strabane Canal linked up with the River Foyle for over 150 years to carry traffic into Strabane. As I mentioned earlier, the Marquis of Abercorn supported the local traders in the building of the 4 mile waterway from Leck near Ballymagorry into the centre of the town in the 1790s. As a result Strabane became one of the busiest places in Northern Ireland, with ships of up to 300 tons sailing the Foyle to and from Derry. The cross-channel schooners coming up the river in full sail must have been a majestic sight. A later development was the convoy of barges towed by the tug Shamrock that commuted daily to Derry Quay with various commodities. This became affectionately known as the Strabane Fleet – always a talking point in Derry of the time. And the Strabane Fleet is remembered in a well-known local ballad concerning a storm that hit the tug Shamrock out of Derry back in the early 1900s:

'Come all you jolly seamen bold,
That plough the raging main.
Give an ear onto my story,
I'll relate to you the same.
Our Shamrock boat moved slowly off,
From Derry we did go.

The River Foyle

Canal Lock, Strabane

*An' at 6 o' clock that very night
The stormy winds did blow…'*

The ballad goes on to tell how one man was lost as the tug was buffeted all the way up the river, with no respite until they reached Port Hall. The tale brought fame to the Fleet, which continued to ply the river for many years after. But then sadly with the introduction of the railways, the Strabane Canal went out of business. However, you can still see part of this unique waterway by taking the A5 road to Ballymagorry and dropping down towards the river's right bank. Here, two fine new locks have been installed. It's an exceptional piece of work and part of the attempt to restore the canal to its former glory. Hopefully one day this historic route will once more make its way to Strabane.

Back on the A5 road I cross the Burn Dennet Bridge. The Dennet is a small stream that flows from the Tyrone Hills – really the tail-end of the Sperrins – through the little village of Donemana, which is almost 6 miles inland. While the locality is famed for its prowess in cricket I'm sure the locals wouldn't mind giving way to a story of romance at nearby Liscloon. It's often referred to as The Case of the Vanishing Lover. These days the melancholic ruins of Ogilby Castle, really a gothic pile that rather resembles a film set, is testament to this unusual yarn, which is recalled in some haunting lines:

*'There is a castle at Liscloon,
Where lovers met and hearts entwined,
Only to leave a memory – a tragedy in parting.
Whispers the wind across the hill, a dying gust, an eerie chill.*

Liscloon

*'Tis silent now under the moon,
The empty castle at Liscloon.'*

The story goes that the son of a well-to-do local family fell in love with a farmer's daughter. The two lovers met in secret by the Dennet Burn and sometimes exchanged notes, which tradition says they placed in an abandoned owl's nest in a tree nearby – the so called Owl's Nest Tree. But, the course of true love never runs smoothly and unfortunately for the young man his mother discovered his liaison with the girl. When he refused to stop seeing her the unrelenting mama had him packed off post-haste to America. To all intents and purposes it seemed that he had vanished from the face of the earth. Understandably the girl was heartbroken and for the next few years wandered the highways and byways of Donemana dressed as in mourning. Then, I suppose as in many a good love story, out of the blue her young lover turned up to claim her. The pair wed straightaway and left for Australia never to see Ireland again.

The name of the young man was James Douglas Ogilby and fittingly enough he met his sweetheart Mary Jane Jamieson on Altnacrees (The Hill of my Heart) just outside the village. Ogilby went on to become a famous zoologist in Australia, with posts in Sydney and Queensland museums, and with many species named after him. He had been a Winchester College schoolboy and later attended Trinity College Dublin to complete his studies. Ogilby was also a magnificent athlete and interestingly enough he cut his teeth in zoology with research carried out on the River Foyle.

Returning to my travels on the Foyle's right bank and I notice the river is now growing much wider – I'd say between a quarter of a mile and half a mile in places. It's worth pausing here to view the surrounding landscape, which now begins to take in an ever-widening panorama of hills on both sides of the river. To the left in the distance are the mountains of north west Donegal, while the low hills directly opposite on the far bank separate the Foyle from Lough Swilly, and they take the eye northwards to the curved arc of the Inishowen Hills. From where I stand on the right bank the terrain rises gradually back into Tyrone and the foothills of the Sperrins.

The colours vary from bluish purple in the distance in Donegal to a staggering range of greens nearer hand, which now in spring are interspersed with great swathes of yellow gorse. Another effect here is when the low evening sun in the west casts its rays into the distant Sperrins – the shoulders of the hills become luminescent and stand out in relief against the darker valleys giving a most magical character to the landscape.

The River Foyle

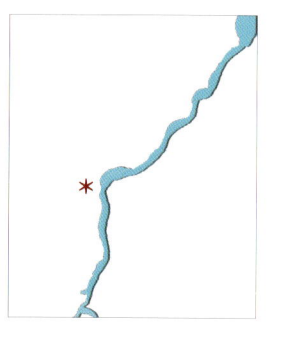

The Foyle at St Johnston

St Johnston

Both sides of the Foyle have rich arable land, but where the river starts to bend to the left sand banks and mud flats are much in evidence at low tides. There's a great fishing tradition on both banks of the river on this stretch and a few tales of poaching that are better left untold. At the same time the whole fishing scene is changing due to restrictions placed on net fishing that have been introduced in a bid to preserve salmon stocks. But the question is will the river ever return to the glory days when the Foyle was considered one of the top European salmon rivers? People hereabouts remember when fish caught at this spot were in London's Billingsgate market the following morning.

My next destination is near the little village of Bready, which is on the A5 road just 6 miles from Derry. I reach a spot on the river known locally as Dunnalong. In the 16th century (c. 1560) it was originally the base of an O'Neill chieftain, who believed that it had a strategic position since there was an important ferry crossing here and good views of the river in each direction. Later, in 1600, on the orders of Elizabeth I, Sir Henry Docwra arrived in the Foyle with ships and troops. He realised the potential of Dunnalong and built an extensive star-shaped fort as a base to wage attacks on the local clans. Historian William Roulston gives an excellent account of this fort in the *Fair Valley River*. Eventually, when hostilities died down Dunnalong fell into decline. Meanwhile Docwra busied himself with building the new Derry near the site of the old monastic settlement. And in fact he is credited with being the second founder of the city – the first being Columcille.

Derry is not yet in sight down river but straight across on the left bank is St Johnston – a village once much involved with salmon fishing. Apart from the fact that there was a ferry here I've also read that there may have been fords across the Foyle in these parts. Mind you that's difficult to believe when you see the width and rapid flow of the river. Certainly at very low tides and in hot summers when the Foyle itself is low the sand banks and mud flats are clearly visible quite the whole way across. But a local man told me no matter how far down the river level goes there's always a narrow channel out in the middle. None the less cattle were taken over long ago and this was usually done by binding their legs and laying them flat in boats – I actually saw this some years ago in vessels crossing from Rathlin Island to the mainland.

Talk of a ferry brings to mind another question. You'll recall that we left Archbishop Colton setting out for Derry after a cool reception at Leckpatrick – I'm wondering did he cross over at this point? You see the old route into Derry in ancient days was mainly down the left bank of the River Foyle. All of which begs the question how did they manage

The River Foyle

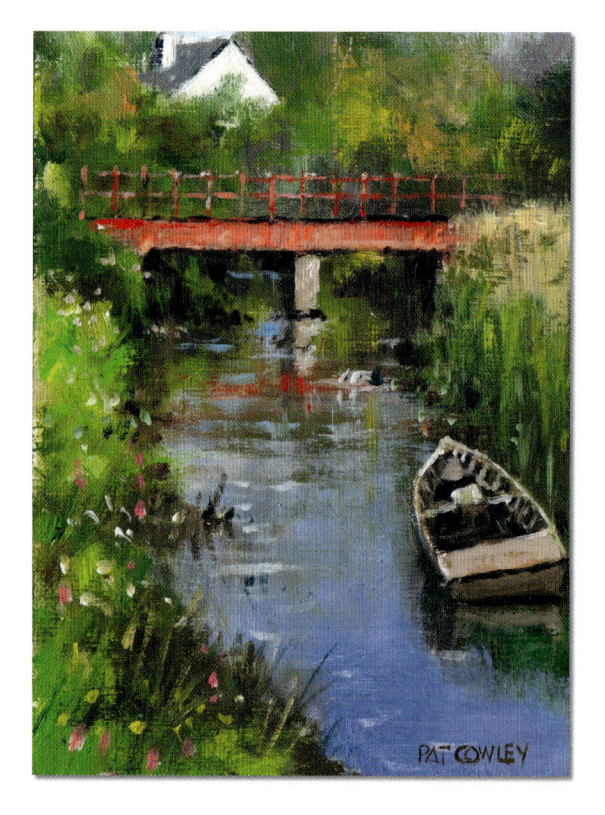

The Boathole, St Johnston

their horses? I wonder did they swim them across behind the ferry boats?

I cannot leave St Johnston without telling a grisly tale that has been handed down as The Legend of Stumpie's Brae. It's a story of greed, of the devil and of a haunting. Stumpie's Brae is about a mile or so outside the village of St Johnston and I decide to travel to the left bank of the Foyle to see the setting for myself. The brae is really only a slope on a narrow, tree-lined road, but there was once was a farm cottage here that saw a weird visitor on a dark and stormy evening. It seems that a strange looking pedlar called and asked the farmer and his wife if he could have a bed for the night. The sly couple watched as he counted his day's takings – a purse full of sovereigns. Then, when he slept they killed him and danced with delight as they seized his gold. In a bid to hide the body they emptied his sack of his possessions and put him into it. When his legs wouldn't fit they promptly chopped them off before dumping the remains out in the bog at the top of the brae.

But just about midnight as they settled down to sleep they thought they heard an odd noise – it was the sound of something slithering as if on two stumps and it was making its way round and round the cottage. Suddenly there was a roar, *"I'll haunt ye high an' I'll haunt ye low down all the days were e'r ye do go!"* It was the pedlar's ghost, thereafter christened Stumpie. And true to his word he haunted the farmer and his wife for the rest of their days – even to America where they fled to escape him.

Incidentally, we owe the story of Stumpie's Brae to none other than the hymn writer Cecil Francis Alexander who came upon the details on one of her excursions into the countryside around the Foyle. She later wrote a poem about it with some very scary opening lines:

'Have ye ever heird o' Stumpie's Brae,
Jist there bi the Foyle where a cottage lay?
Come closer tae me wan an' aw,
Till I tell ye how the de'il did caw.'

Maybe it's just because of the spooky tale but I find Stumpie's Brae a very oppressive place and soon set out for the nearby village of Carrigans. It's about a mile away and not far from the border with Northern Ireland. This little community found itself in the national headlines in 1938 when there were three mysterious shootings within an hour in the old world mansion of the McClintock family just outside the village. In 1924 Colonel Robert McClintock returned from India to manage the estate, with his wife Jennie and their only son William aged 11. Fourteen years later, on Saturday 24 September 1938 William, who had been paralysed in a riding accident, was discovered shot dead in the walled garden. Shortly afterwards his mother was found dead outside the garden near a tool shed and again as the result of a gunshot wound. Minutes later William's bride to be, society girl Helen Mackworth, was found shot dead beside the body of her lover. That evening a hastily convened inquest concluded that the mother had shot her son and then herself while the balance of her mind was disturbed. Similarly, Helen Mackworth was adjudged to have shot herself.

The newspapers covered the story with headlines such as *'Death in a Donegal Mansion'* and ever since people have wondered about the many weird contradictions in the details that have emerged about the Dunmore episode. Some likened it to an Agatha Christie whodunnit. Imagine the surprise then when it was revealed that Jennie McClintock's first cousin was Archie Christie, married to this self same Agatha. In a further bizarre twist it also turned out that Agatha Christie had in fact visited Dunmore with Archie's brother, the writer, Campbell Christie. Perhaps the strangest thing of all is the inscription on Jennie's gravestone:

Rest after toil
Port after stormy seas

Astonishing as it seems this quote from the Elizabethan poet Spenser also turns up on the gravestone of Agatha Christie.

Visiting Dunmore I discover that it too was designed by Michael Priestley – the second of his four houses along the river. I am fortunate to be able to visit both the house and the walled garden where young McClintock was shot. Externally the dwelling looks like a large Irish manor house. Sitting on a rise above a tree-lined meadow it is finished in

The River Foyle

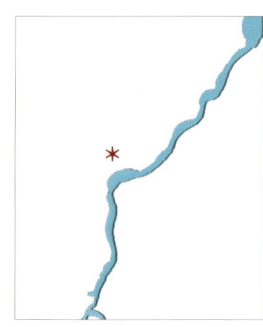

The River Foyle from the hills above Carrigans

Newbuildings

grey stucco with an attractive central Venetian style window. My first impression is that it has nothing of the look of the usual Priestley architecture. However, inside I find the staircase to be in his style and it lends a gracious touch to the entire house, which is bright and handsomely furnished.

From the upstairs windows roughly a mile away you can see the Foyle about to begin its straight wide run into Derry. If you were in a boat on the river at this stage you'd see the first signs of the city. Island like, it rises up out of the distant haze dominated by the outline of the spire of St Columb's Church of Ireland Cathedral against the sky. You can clearly see how the river flowed on each side of Derry in ancient times and I rate this as one of the most spectacular approaches to any city I have visited.

Less than three miles out from Derry the terrain is now steeper on both sides of the river. Over on the right bank near the water's edge you can see the village of Newbuildings. It owes its roots to the Plantation and was part of the Goldsmith's domain. The village was an important fishing station in times past and a remarkable story is told about a memorable night in 1895. Apparently the river glistened from one side to the other when a massive shoal of salmon came up with the incoming tide. There was an eerie noise as hundreds upon hundreds of fish thrashed about and for ages the water seemed to be boiling. Yet times move on and the great days of fishing at Newbuildings and the night that salmon filled the Foyle all the way across are only a memory now.

I stay with the left bank where there is a riverside walk along the route of the old GNR railway, whose bridges I've seen further back along the system. On the slope above me is Government House – a Victorian villa style residence built in 1847 for the agent of The Honourable The Irish Society – the group much involved with the administration of Derry after the Plantation. Later in 1916 the Irish writer Lord Dunsany stayed here along with the renowned poet Francis Ledwidge. They were in the army and stationed at Ebrington Barracks in the Waterside district of the city. Ledwidge, who was sometimes called 'The Poet of the Blackbirds', had a great sense of the outdoors and things rustic, with perhaps a touch of melancholy and foreboding. Lord Dunsany wrote the introduction to Ledwidge's second book of poetry while in Derry and the following year during World War I the poet was killed near Ypres. Happily his work is now experiencing a much deserved renaissance. A reminder of this poet who would have gazed on the Foyle from the slope above the river comes with his own words that appear on his memorial:

He shall not hear the bittern cry
In the wild sky where he is lain.

The River Foyle

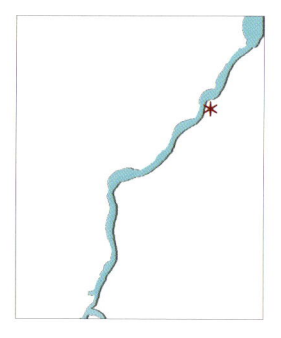

Looking southwards up the Foyle from above the Waterside

Prehen

Nor voices of the sweeter birds,
Above the wailing of the wind.

On the right bank of the Foyle opposite Government House is the townland of Prehen (Preachan – Place of the Crows). Until 1929 the woods here were believed to contain the last of the great oaks of Derry, or at least their ancestors. Then most of them were cut down. Through the remaining trees you can just about see Prehen House. This impressive dwelling is very much wrapped up in the history of Derry – there are stories of sadness here but of great happiness as well. Prehen House is Georgian in style – the third of the four on the river bank built by Michael Priestley – and it has everything of the architect's style – a very pronounced Gibbsian entrance door, with similar windows and corners, and the usual distinctive staircase and generous Georgian windows.

The abode belonged to Andrew Knox MP for Donegal and it was at Prehen in 1757 that 15 year old Mary Ann Knox, the daughter of the family, met the dashing and debonair John McNaughten. He was heavily in debt due to gambling and tradition holds that he wanted to marry Mary Ann for her dowry. Another version of the story says they were deeply in love and that they went through a version of the marriage ceremony in secret. Naturally, Andrew Knox was enraged when he discovered this and McNaughten was banned from Prehen. In response, in November 1761, he lay in wait for the Knox coach as it made its way to Dublin, hoping to snatch Mary Ann. The poor girl was mortally wounded in the resulting fracas and John McNaughten, still declaring that he loved her, found himself languishing in Lifford jail. As we saw earlier, having jumped off the gallows twice, he will forever be remembered as Half-hanged McNaughten since that fateful day in 1761.

Much later in 1910, a young German – Baron Von Scheffler – inherited the Prehen estate from his grandfather Colonel George Knox. This was the beginning of further sadness at Prehen. The house, its treasures and furnishings and over 3000 acres of land were seized by the British government

Prehen House

The River Foyle

during World War I because Von Scheffler was a German. In fact he was put under house arrest and escaped. Eventually, everything was sold off and the woods cut down for building. In the succeeding years there were times when the old dwelling was empty and more or less open to the elements. But then happier days returned in 1972 when Julian and Carola Peck, relatives of the Knox family, bought the house back and restored it to its former Georgian splendour. It took decades to achieve but in 2008 their efforts were rewarded premier status (Grade A) as a historic building. Prehen House, sitting above the Foyle's right bank, is now an invaluable source of times past in Georgian Derry – open to all, it is also an excellent educational resource for schools.

The journey has now taken me to the outskirts of Derry. Looking down river from either bank you can see the formidable Craigavon Bridge – the only double–deck road bridge in Europe. Completed in 1933, it links the main part of the city, which is on the west bank of the river, to the Waterside district on the east bank. This bridge is quarter of a mile in length so it gives you an idea of the width of the Foyle here. It's also between 30 and 40 feet in depth depending on the tides. An earlier bridge also crossed at this spot – Carlisle Bridge was made of iron and was in use from 1863 until the bigger Craigavon Bridge was built. Carlisle Bridge was associated with what became known in those early days as the 'Mysterious Malady'. During construction in 1861 five men working inside the metal caissons down on the river bed became gravely ill and died. The caissons were iron cylinders that would later become support pillars, but during operations they were filled with compressed air. Unknown to the builders the men had died of Decompression Sickness or Caisson Sickness, commonly called the bends. This was one of the early episodes of the disease amongst bridge builders.

Derry's first bridge crossed the river 100 yards further downstream. A wooden structure, it was built seventy years earlier by a Boston firm with experience of constructing bridges over fast-flowing, wide rivers. It was partly assembled in America and brought to Derry on ships along with massive oak uprights that were strapped to the sides of the vessels. This bridge, which opened in 1791, had a chequered history – there were rows with the existing ferry company, arguments about the cost of tolls, and a drawbridge was needed to allow vessels to sail upstream to the Strabane Canal. At one stage Derry's wooden bridge was washed away and in the end in its rickety state I think it must have taken nerves of steel to cross it.

Of course the need to provide a crossing over the Foyle in the 18th century meant that the city was growing – a link to the developing Waterside district was called for – also, there was increasing traffic into and out of Derry. Up to the mid-

Bridges over the Foyle at Derry

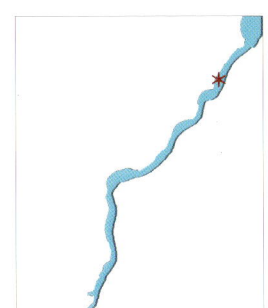

The Island of Derry

91

The River Foyle

1700s the main approach to the city from the south was down the left bank of the river from Lifford along the River Foyle – back in 1689 this was the route that the army of James II took. It was a winding torturous journey. However, a new bridge over the River Mourne at Strabane in the early 1700s meant that traffic from Derry could now also take the right bank and this in fact was the way the Knox coach travelled when Mary Ann was murdered in 1761. Then in 1795 a new road out of Waterside along the river by Prehen meant that the right bank became the preferred route for most coaches going south through Strabane, Omagh and Newtownstewart towards Dublin. People wanting to get to Derry from Belfast in those times came by Coleraine and Newtown Limavady. This involved taking a road from a northerly direction along the right bank of the Foyle. Travellers would then take the ferry across to the city. After 1791, when the wooden bridge came into service, this route became much busier.

Talking of these old routes, many of which were full of pot holes until the 1800s, it seems that the great and the good always wanted to visit Derry regardless of the hazards. Why you might ask? Well firstly the tour of Ireland became an almost obligatory thing for writers, historians and reformers of one sort or another in the 18th and 19th centuries – Derry at the top of the island fitted nicely into the circuit. Secondly, Derry was of special interest because of the Siege in 1689 and people also wanted to know about education, living conditions and poverty, in this city that was at the north western edge of Europe.

As you might expect the visitor's comments were many and varied. Arriving in Derry after the Spanish Armada the feisty Spanish Captain Francisco de Quellar wasn't impressed by the rough local men but liked the women a lot. Sometime later, Arthur Young, the agricultural reformer, coming to visit his friend the Earl of Bristol in 1776, found Derry picturesque but was none too pleased that he had to wait two hours for a ferry. And he was much less pleased when he found the Earl Bishop was away on one of his frequent European tours. In 1796 the Frenchman De Lacotayne found Derry charming and told the story of how the Polish dwarf Count Boralaski was lifted and placed upon the hotel mantelpiece by his wife after they'd had a row. This Boralaski was 26 inches tall, fathered 7 children and lived to be 97 years of age.

Writer William Makepiece Thackeray had a rare old time dining out in Derry in 1842 but felt his hotel resembled a cemetery and grumbled about the waiters and post-boys looking for tips. In 1847 historian Lord Macaulay in a more upbeat manner praised Derry's walls, while the great essayist Thomas Carlyle pronounced Derry to be pretty yet felt the new railway along the River Foyle to Coleraine was a disaster. But by far the greatest fury was reserved for a Derry customs man in 1902. Traveller Samuel Bayne had just arrived by boat from America to commence his jaunting car tour of the west of Ireland when the zealous official pounced. He even seized a half-used packet of cigarettes and made the ladies shake out their dresses in case anything was concealed. All of which left Bayne with an experience of Derry best forgotten.

And what of recent times? Modern travel writer Dervla Murphy said of Derry – *'I found some ancient spell being laid on me…'* And I think that is very much the way I think of it myself. When you see Derry with the great sweep of the River Foyle, and the city stretching up the hillsides on each bank and all of this set against the magnificent, almost hypnotic, Donegal hills, a spell is cast. Somehow you get a sense both of a thriving community but also one that is still graced with the antique. And for me there is not the slightest doubt that the River Foyle is at the heart of it. Having spent a lifetime writing and broadcasting about Derry it seems to me that the river is inextricably linked with this place and the lives of the people around it.

In thinking about this I see the Foyle at the centre of what you might call coming and going. First there came Columcille (Dove of the Church). In 546 AD he was gifted Doire Calgach (Calgach's Oak Grove, or Derry) by a kinsman and thus Derry began – the Island in the River Foyle. But, almost in the manner of a Greek tragedy, as if destined to happen, he exiled himself by way of the river that he loved – it was a sacrifice and a very symbolic act in the story of the Saint.

Moving on to the Middle Ages, with Derry still an island in the centre of the river. At dusk on October 1397 I envisage Archbishop Colton and his entourage having travelled up along the river now hailing the ferry-man on the island, most likely from a spot on the left bank roughly opposite the Long Tower Church in the Derry of today. When they eventually crossed to what was now Derry Columcille, members of the Cathedral Chapter, which included administrators and cannons, were missing from the welcoming party. It was something that spelt major trouble and meant that Colton and his party could be at considerable risk. You see Derry had no bishop at the time and the Chapter was in effect part of the ruling the community.

Over the next four days Colton's diary reveals the crisis and indeed the mystery surrounding Derry. Firstly, the Chapter members and a privileged few, including local rulers, were keeping all the monies earned from the church lands for themselves. Secondly, the monks responsible for the nearby Black Abbey of St Columba were living openly in the monastery with women and their children. The entire commu-

The River Foyle

nity had become lax and dissolute. It also turned out that one of the monks had usurped the authority of the abbot by seizing the mysterious symbolic seal. This was usually kept in a chest that could only be opened by the keys of three separate trustees. By tradition the guardian of the seal held sway in the monastery. So something strange was going on – there was intrigue in the monastery of the island city.

Although the riddle of what was really happening may never be solved, one thing was certain – Derry was in decline. Yet Colton won the day by the subtle art of divide and conquer and clever diplomacy – he also threatened mass excommunication and everyone knew he could resort to force as he had done elsewhere. So with a cobbled together agreement Archbishop Colton left the island of Derry on 14th October 1397. He travelled down the river a short distance before turning inland to Dunvigen. From there he travelled up into the Sperrins and eventually met the top of the Glenelly Valley not far from where we first encountered his party on the first part of our journey. He had achieved his Derry mission but thereafter vanished into history dying seven years later in 1404.

Derry saw substantial incursions by the Normans between the 12th and 14th centuries. Yet it was almost 200 years after Colton that the river witnessed fundamental changes that were to leave lasting imprints. Colonisation from England had commenced. It all started in 1566 with an expeditionary force from Britain coming up the Foyle and settling around the old monastery on the island. Three years later this foray was gradually petering out but it came to an abrupt end after a powder magazine stored nearby in the ancient Templemore Cathedral exploded. It marked the demise of this venerable old building but not the end of English interest in the potential of the Foyle. Elizabeth I wanted garrisons along the river and in 1600 Sir Henry Docwra set out to fulfil her wishes. This brought forts such as we heard about at Dunnalong near Bready further upstream.

A map of the time shows that Derry was still an island in the centre of the Foyle. However, the western channel was beginning to silt up – this later became Bogside as it is today. And while Docwra's interest waned, over the next two decades the Stuart King, James I, would accelerate what came to be called the Plantation – the systematic redistribution and re-populating of Irish lands. James gave the Livery Companies of London responsibility for the Plantation of Ulster and one of their chief tasks was the building of the new city of Derry. In fact it also got a new name – in March 1613, to mark its association with the capital, Derry was changed to Londonderry by Charter. Later the company chosen to manage affairs here was given the title of The Honourable The Irish Society. This body still exists today in a philanthropic capacity.

The Island of Derry

Looking up into the city from the Bay Road

The River Foyle

It is with the Irish Society that we see the Foyle and its tributaries becoming commercial, especially with respect to salmon fishing. And of course the river, always the main means of communication, was now continually busy with ships bringing soldiers, skilled workers, families, produce and materials.

In 1689 the Foyle was in the thick of things even more with the comings and goings at the Siege of Derry. A much commemorated event, this was the third and biggest of such attacks since 1600 and it lasted 105 days. Derry, as it was then, lay on the eastern slope of the old island facing the river. It was oval-shaped and had a very antique feel about it, with its half-timbered houses and perimeter of solid stone walls lined with cannons. The circuit of the walls was barely a mile long – it averaged 20 feet in width and 20 feet in height. It's a staggering thought that 30,000 people were packed in here at the start of the siege, behind these stout defences. And today those self-same walls are still intact. The cannons have had a facelift and Derry can boast that it is one of the finest walled cities in Europe and still have a reminder of the warring days of the 1600s.

For the Foyle it was to be the 1700s before the river really took centre stage in the development of the north west of Ireland. This came about for a number of reasons. Firstly, after some decades in Ireland many Presbyterians who'd come from Scotland were finding it difficult to eke out a satisfactory existence here, and they were also barred from holding official posts. These Ulster-Scots, as they've been called, saw better opportunities in America and the natural outlet was through Derry Quay and the Foyle. It has to be added that the exodus also contained people from the Established Church but the majority were Presbyterians.

Secondly, as Derry started to grow there was a greater demand for materials, foodstuffs, and even luxury items, so ships were coming and going to all parts of the world. Thirdly, this growing activity along the waterway created a further industry in shipping repairs and the supply of all the other commodities needed for a thriving port. In modern parlance Derry was buzzing thanks to the river. And this continued throughout the 1800s, for when the initial outpouring of the Ulster-Scots dropped away a second wave of emigration commenced, this time mainly native Irish caught in the grip of impossible conditions during and after a succession of famines.

So the River Foyle saw thousands of emigrants going and empty ships returning to collect more. Yet folk leaving Derry were fortunate for in these days of the so-called 'coffin ships' the vessels from here were generally in good condition. The McCorkell line was by far the biggest owner of sailing ships along Derry Quay. The founder, William Mc-

Emigration from Derry

Corkell, who'd been a supporter of Bonnie Prince Charlie, originally had fled Scotland. The story goes that he rowed to Ireland by boat with his two brothers. Eventually, he set up his shipping company in 1778. Trade flourished and by the mid-1800s his grandson Barry had gained an intimate knowledge of the shipping business and owned a massive fleet of sailing ships.

Many of the vessels had Indian names such as *Hiawatha*, *Minnehaha* and *Nokomis* and people often wonder why this was so. The answer is that Barry McCorkell's father sent him to sea to learn the trade and while he was travelling along the eastern seaboard of America he encountered the great poet H. W. Longfellow. It's possible that he may have visited Craigie House, the Longfellow home in Massachusetts. Whatever the case, so taken was he with the famous man that he began to name his ships after characters in the epic poem *Hiawatha* – the greatest being the clipper *Minnehaha*, which served the McCorkell line for 35 years. The *Minnehaha* was a Derry favourite and folks lined the banks of the Foyle to see her arrivals and departures.

In those times Derry Quay was thronged with emigrants, traders, pedlars, seamen, workers and even smugglers – and there were hundreds of people just standing around observing the hustle and bustle of the milling crowds. Along the waterfront sailing ships were tied up five abreast and you can imagine the trauma of departure. These partings were called 'Yankee Wakes' and often a lone fiddler would strike up as the ships cast off. And for those from Donegal who could not bear to see their loved ones off at Derry there was a little bridge near Muckish Mountain where painful farewells were made. Emigrants then crossed the bridge on their own before waving their final goodbyes. This bridge lives on poignantly as the 'Bridge of Tears'.

And in Derry itself the heartbreak of a young man who had to leave his sweetheart to search for work in America is told in the following lines:

'Farewell to Derry and to you my love.
I look my last, my love,
At places where we walked, talked,
And promised never parting.
And so I leave my spirit in these hills and vales,
To meet your's on a summer morn.
I fear I shall not find you…
Will you not whisper on the breeze…a little sigh?
This barque is moving on my love,
As Foyle swings seaward.
New World beckons without you.
Where now, my love? Where now…?'

The River Foyle

The Derry of those days of the 1800s consisted of the inner city surrounded by a sprawl of cabins and little houses outside the walls – many people had come in from the local countryside and from Donegal in the hope of finding employment. But work was scarce and it was to be the middle of the century before conditions began to improve. Around the 1860s you find new streets, new houses, and new industries adding to the continuing boom at the port. Several streets containing the big Victorian terrace houses used by the shipping folk still exist today.

As for enterprises, the city had a linen hall until trade switched to Belfast. Watts Distillery probably became the biggest whiskey producer in the world; shipbuilding flourished on the riverfront, and shirt-making became Derry's stock in trade, with thousands of women employed. One thing I marvel at is the number of smaller industries that existed in those days – rope and glass works, bacon curing, brewing, sugar refining and tobacco, to mention but a few of the many. And in much of this the river played a vital role in that ships of considerable tonnage could bring in raw materials and take away goods and produce.

And in today's Derry after 30 years of the 'Troubles' it's as if a renaissance is in prospect. There are new developments all around the city and great attempts are being made to convert the Siege walls into a tourist attraction and a unique educational resource. Derry also boasts two fine cathedrals in contrasting Gothic styles – St Columb's Church of Ireland and St Eugene's Catholic. And there are some fine examples of 19th century architecture in the churches of other denominations. Yet for such a historic location you cannot find too many places where the city has a Georgian feel, or even a Victorian feel. It makes me ponder whether the developers in the early 1900s just built where the opportunity presented itself, without much attention to what should have been preserved – to what would have given the city more architectural character. And what on earth took possession of the city fathers in those bygone days when they changed the beautiful names of Silver Street and Gracious Street into plain Shipquay Street and Ferryquay Street?

To the journey again, which has now taken me down the river's left bank past Craigavon Bridge and on to Derry Quay devoid of trading ships that have been moved to a port further down stream. Just below Craigavon Bridge the river curves gently to the left and then commences a long swing to the right. This really is the heart of Derry – marked by the town hall, or the Guildhall – a gothic style edifice in red sandstone, whose clock tower dominates the city centre. On the opposite bank is the new Ilex enterprise, where the former army garrison of Ebrington (1841) is being developed into a modern business complex. The flow of the river

Buzzing Derry

here is swift and the water light brown in colour but not clear as in upper parts of the system.

When you think about it, in the space of 1000 years the ships of the Danes and the Normans have been here, ships of the English, emigrant ships, and later the ships of two world wars.

The last of these, World War II, saw the river in one of the busiest and most colourful phases of its history. Derry, with its harbour on the north west edge of Europe, suddenly had a strategic role in the defence of the North Atlantic. As a result vessels from all over the world came up the Foyle for repairs, or to allow fatigued servicemen have a break. Soon it seemed that nearly every nationality in the world was walking Derry streets.

There were British and American bases here and Russia accents were heard for the first time. Romances, friendships, brawls in local bars and even an upturn in the local economy all stemmed from the new arrivals on the River Foyle. And the stars of the day – Bob Hope, Al Jolson, the Andrews Sisters and many more came to entertain the hundreds of young Americans stationed here. Derry actually featured in one movie afterwards – *The Gift Horse* – made in 1952. And even when the war was over the city and its river still continued to function as a NATO base until the early 1960s.

So the Foyle more or less saw a constant and massive presence of ships for decades after 1900. Yet sadly, all that has changed now.

These days the emptiness of Derry Quay is palpable. For a mile and a half the great curve of one of the finest waterways in the world has an air of melancholy about it, set as it is against the beauty of the rising hills on each side. It's as if everyone and everything has sailed away. Mind you when sailing boats, or liners, come up to visit these days the atmosphere of the whole place is transformed and uplifted. Other than that only one river cruiser plies the Foyle, with trips for sightseers. I think it was Ovid who said *'Time is the devourer of all things'*, and you have to ask will the life of former days ever return to this part of the river? I suppose the other thing you have to wonder about is what are the stories left untold – of loss, of heartbreak, of intrigue, of love and of valour too, for the Foyle has surely moulded the destiny of many a man and woman.

One such tale was told to me by a veteran sea captain as we sat overlooking the river from a height on the right bank. He came into Derry in 1942 for ship repairs and fell head over heels in love with the girl sent to fetch him to the naval HQ. She promised to wait for him until the war was over and there she was on Derry Quay to greet him 3 years later, as she'd said. They were married straightaway in a match

The River Foyle

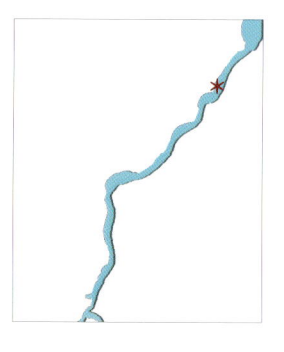

The city from the Waterside

that lasted 40 years. He also recalled how as a child he was lifted up to wave goodbye to his father, who was leaning over the deck rail of a great ship pulling away from Southampton. That vessel was the *Titanic* and strangely the loss of his father in 1912 spurred him on to run away to sea at the age of 14. He had sailed every ocean in the world before he came up the River Foyle to find his sweetheart and make his home in Derry.

It's on the left bank in the centre of the city that you really discover just how much Derry lies in a valley dominated by the Foyle and the surrounding hills. Downstream on the Donegal side are two spectacular round top mountains – Scalp and Eskaheen. Above the city itself is Creggan Hill, and further back to the south Sherriff's mountain and Holywell Hill. On the right bank directly opposite in Waterside the rising ground that eventually takes you to the north eastern end of the Sperrins is called Clondermott Hill – a name you don't find used much nowadays. Nearby, you can't miss Corrody and Kittybane. These two hills along with Creggan Hill offer the best views of Derry and the River Foyle from on high as it were.

Most panoramas of Derry for television, movies, or postcards are taken from the Corrody area, and this reminds me of 3 seasonal skies over Derry and the Foyle that I find highly pleasing. The first is in late October looking west from the height above the Waterside. As the sun sinks behind the Donegal hills on clear evenings the sky takes on a deep copper hue with the spires of the churches and rooftops set out in black silhouette against it. Upstream to the south the wide coppery curve of the river casts a strange luminous patina over the landscape giving a unique vista mainly only seen in the autumn. The second comes on winter mornings when frosty pink and grey clouds blow in over the river against an intense blue sky that looks to be straight out of a Claude Lorraine painting. And the third is looking north west from Corrody in settled weather where the Foyle swings out of the city past Scalp Mountain. Set against a clear summer sky the slopes come into relief with rich darker hues of green, purple, beige and yellow, as the growth takes hold – a scene all the more attractive when the shadows of clouds drift slowly across.

At the end of Derry Quay you meet a little bulge in the river called Rosses Bay. The railway to Coleraine and Belfast follows the right bank northwards and now before you is the Foyle Bridge, Derry's second and most modern bridge. It was opened in 1984 and is one of the highest and longest bridges in Ireland. The Foyle Bridge actually consists of 2 separate carriageways and the centre spans were floated up the river before being lifted into place. The view southwards up the river towards the city from this bridge is spectacular

The River Foyle

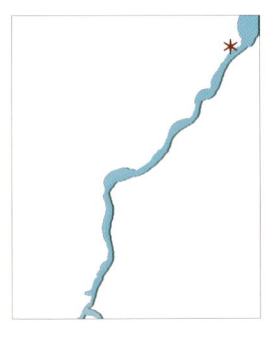

The Docks at Lisahally

Boom Hall

– looking northwards down stream the stretch below you is known as the 'Narrows' – some 60 feet deep.

Just past the bridge on the left bank, through the trees you get a sight of the ruin of a house known as Boom Hall. Set in several acres of meadows and trees Boom Hall goes back to the days of great Derry houses. As we shall see shortly the name derives from a boom placed across the river here during the Siege in 1689. And Boom Hall is the last of the Michael Priestley houses along the river. Now without its roof and looking rather sorry for itself I feel it must have been the most modern of Priestley's designs. Sadly, there was a fire here in 1972 so now there is nothing inside save crumbling walls. Yet from the elegant façade it must have been a magnificent dwelling in its day. It was the home of the Alexander family from 1779 – the same line as the famous army general Earl Alexander of Tunis and Bishop William Alexander the former Protestant Primate of Ireland. William's father was born here and William and his wife Cecil Francis Alexander the hymn writer would often have visited Boom Hall and strolled down by the river bank.

I wander around the ruin reflecting on two odd tales concerning the house that we owe to William Alexander. The first is about an 8-year old boy, Waller Alexander, who died while on holiday in Drogheda and was seen at the same instant at Boom Hall. This story of the boy's wraith was firmly believed by all of the family. The second was of a mysterious lady visitor discovered in the grounds near the river. The woman, of foreign origin, was dressed magnificently but could not speak – or preferred not to do so. She was obviously in great distress and the Alexanders provided work and accommodation for her. After a few years and still not speaking she died of what was described as a broken heart – the mystery is still unsolved. One suggestion was that she had been put back on land from a ship leaving Derry for reasons that remain unknown – who knows, perhaps a lover's tiff, or a secret onboard tryst uncovered?

By the way, inland about a mile or so from the river, you find the Amelia Earhart Museum. The pioneering aviatrix landed her *Lockheed Vega* in a field at Ballyarnett on 20 May 1932 after her record breaking solo flight across the Atlantic from Newfoundland. In my early days as a broadcaster I interviewed some of the people who'd remembered seeing Amelia as she frantically searched for a place to land after her 15 hour flight. James McGeady told me how he watched as the wheels of the plane clipped the tree beside his house before she landed. "Can you tell me where I am?" was Amelia's first question. Another man saw her come in over the river and circle so low above him that he thought he'd have to run for cover. Amelia said afterwards that she'd followed the railway line along the Foyle hoping it would lead to a town. It did, and of course the town was Derry. Overnight the

The River Foyle

news of the first woman to fly the Atlantic solo hit the world headlines and the field where Amelia landed was thronged with thousands of visitors. Amelia's aircraft was packed into crates and both the plane and Amelia were spirited away the following day having found a niche for themselves in the annals of flight pioneering on the banks of the River Foyle.

To the river bank once more and you can appreciate why this stretch got the name 'Narrows' for the opposite bank is barely a stone's throw away, especially when the tide is low. It was here during the Siege that a boom consisting of chain and trees was stretched across the river by the forces of James II to prevent relief ships getting up to Derry. And it was the breaking of the boom that brought relief to the besieged city.

A hundred yards further down stream are the remains of the old wooden jetties of Lisahally. A large part of the German submarine fleet surrendered at this very location in 1945. The vessels – 60 in total – were later taken out into the Atlantic and scuttled. Surely something that wouldn't be countenanced in today's world?

It was also at Lisahally that HMS *Amythest,* famed for the Yangtze Incident (1949), was berthed before she was taken away to star in the film of that name. Incidentally, the Foyle was the last river the *Amythest* ever sailed on for shortly afterwards she was accidentally blown up in the making of the movie.

And it's here, between Culmore Point on the left bank and Lisahally on the right bank that the River Foyle flows into Lough Foyle so ending this great river journey. Yet we mustn't forget that the lough too is part of the system and I feel it would be fitting to see where the last stretch of the Foyle enters the ocean. Firstly, a word about the River Faughan (Sheltered Place) that flows in from the right just a few yards past Lisahally. The Faughan winds its way from the northern Sperrins through County Derry down to Lough Foyle. A river of wonderful character it is graced by several big country houses along its length. I'm afraid that time does not permit a trip along the banks of the River Faughan on this occasion. Suffice to say that for its size this little river was one of the most worked waterways in Northern Ireland during the 1800s and early 1900s. You find the remains of countless mills, weirs, floodgates and lades, and the river is tree-lined throughout, with mysterious pools and breathtaking scenery. The River Faughan is famed for its beauty and is steeped in history but we must let it hold its stories for another day.

Lisahally

The River Faughan flowing down from the Eagle's Nest

Lough Foyle

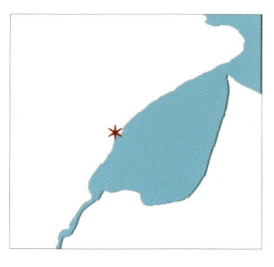

Fishing boats at Quigley's Point

Lough Foyle to the Sea

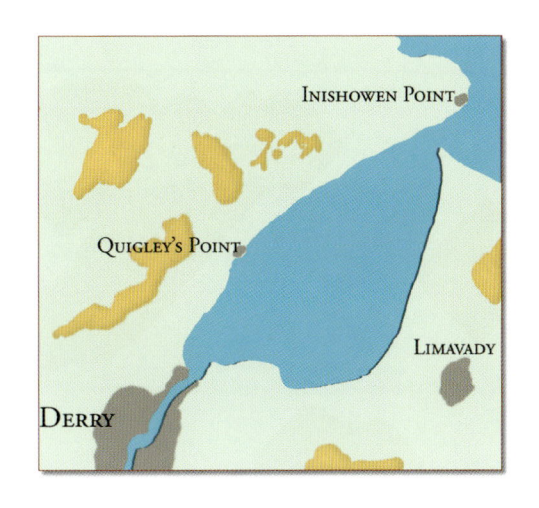

Lough Foyle is oval in shape, being 16 miles long and with widths varying up to 10 miles. It lies in what's known locally as Derry Vale. Bounded by the Inishowen hills on the left and the north western foothills of the Sperrins on the right, it is said to be one of the most scenic spots in Ireland. It is world famous through the song Danny Boy – The Derry, or Londonderry Air. Most credit for the music is given to Jane Ross of Limavady who is believed to have written down the notes of an air played by the fiddler Jimmy McCurry on a market day.

Looking northwards you now get a first glimpse of the sea in the distance where the beach on the right side of Lough Foyle sweeps in a huge arc towards Magilligan Point. As for the flat land around Magilligan one visitor here in the 1820s was none other than George Everest – Mount Everest was called after him. The famous surveyor had taken a break from India to see the experiments of Colonel Thomas Colby, who was preparing for the great Irish Ordnance Sur-

Lough Foyle

vey. Magilligan, near the Foyle shoreline, had been chosen as the Base Line for the whole of Ireland. Astonishingly, the survey itself took almost two decades (1824–1842) and involved not just experts in measurements but also required a vast team of map makers, engravers, historians and folklorists. The Ordnance Survey is a key point in Irish history. At 6 inches to the mile Ireland was mapped in a way hitherto unknown. It also saw the invention of compensation bars and the development of limelight. A troop of soldiers was needed to haul giant theodolites up the mountain-sides and when the survey for an area was complete, Colby would hold a plum pudding feast on the last measured peak for all his men.

As I noted back at the River Strule, John O'Donovan was invited to join the survey on account of his expertise in the Irish language. The idea was to have a Memoir of every parish in Ireland but the project was eventually shelved – leaving the famous 'paper mountain', including O'Donovan's papers and letters, at the Survey's HQ in Pheonix Park, Dublin. For the record the Derry Memoir was the only one ever produced.

From Magilligan Point it is only a mile across the water to the port of Greencastle directly opposite in Donegal on the left side of the estuary. On the right side you see the striking basalt cliffs of Benevenagh that guard the entrance to Lough Foyle. This spot, where the Foyle enters the Atlantic Ocean, is best viewed from the gallery at Gortmore on Benevenagh, which you reach by the Bishop's Road. It took 200 men to build this road in the late 1700s for the Earl Bishop, Frederick Hervey. He wanted a shorter more scenic route to his castle on the Downhill cliffs. Away to the right you can still see the ruin of his 18th century abode on the cliff top and out on the edge is the classical Mussenden Temple. This beautiful edifice was built in honour of the young Fridiswide Mussenden, who some believe was his sweetheart.

On clear days from Gortmore looking north you can see some of the Scottish islands. To the east is the headland at the Giant's Causeway; Portrush is also visible, as is the Bar Mouth of the River Bann. Straight across is Inishowen Head in Donegal, and laid out far below you is the vast triangle of fields that tapers off into Magilligan Point. At most times out in the middle of the channel you will see waves breaking on a sand bank. This is the notorious Tuns Bank. According to mythology the bad-tempered sea god Mananan McLir lives here – the foam-topped waves being his white horses. In reality the 'Tuns' is an extremely dangerous hazard for shipping. There are many sinister stories surrounding this treacherous stretch of sand that appears to boil up into a frenzy on stormy days.

Magilligan Point

The entrance to the Foyle from Inishowen Head

109

Lough Foyle

High up on the cliff top gallery is a fitting place to end the journey. Here the Foyle, having met all the challenges from the hills, the valleys and the plains, finds freedom with its passage to the sea. The book of Ecclesiastes uses the image of the river to the sea – the seemingly endless cycle of flow and replenishment – as a way of describing man's continually yearning, unsatisfied, earthly nature. Certainly the river's flow seems endless – the Foyle is always there – drawing people to it generation after generation and helping to shape their destinies in so many ways – so the cycle continues. I suppose we can say this all started when people first came to inhabit its banks. The ancient name of the waterway is attributed to a Tuatha De Danann prince Feabhail, son of Lodran, who was drowned and washed ashore. This spot was named Feabhail in memory of him – the Anglicised version being Foyle. Another meaning for Loch Feabhail is Estuary of the Lip. And you can see how that came about when you look down from Gortmore at the great spread of the lough narrowing into Magilligan Point.

The journey along the Foyle system has taken me through the months of mid-winter into spring and early summer. Here, where the Foyle enters the sea I recall the many magical places I've seen – and the great stories I've heard along the way. My last look is back up the Lough Foyle towards where the River Foyle flows from those two great valleys in the south that I mentioned at the start of the journey. And although it is the Foyle that I see below, it is also the Strule, the Mourne and the Finn, with their tributaries and the countless burns that have tumbled down the mountains to create this remarkable waterway.

The experience has been memorable, and I must mention Pat Cowley who covered these self-same streams to bring such magnificent images. We chatted much about how to convey impressions of the river but most times over the months our journeys along the banks took us different ways and were solo and challenging with it. Often Pat took the high road and I took the low road and vice versa as we trekked the great Foyle waterway.

So, as we come to the end of our travels we've both agreed that the words of the folk musician Woody Guthrie describe us well:

We've been hittin' some hard travellin' Lord,
We thought you knowed
We've been hittin' some hard travellin', hard rambling…'
We've been hittin' some hard travellin', Lord…
We thought you knowed…

Bibliography

Alexander, E. (ed.) *Primate Alexander Archbishop of Armagh, A Memoir.* Arnold, London 1913

Alexander, C.F. A *The Graveyard in the Hills*

Bayne, S. *On an Irish Jaunting Car through Donegal and Connemara.* (1902)

Bonner, B. Derry: *An Outline History of the Diocese.* FNT, Dublin (1982)

Colby, T. *Ordnance Survey of the County of Londonderry, Vol I,* Hodges and Smith, Dublin (1837).

Carlin, F. The Ballad of Douglas Bridge, in *Anthology of Irish Verse,* P. Colum (1922)

Day, A. and Mc Williams P. (eds.) *Ordnance Survey Memoirs of Ireland, The Parishes of Tyrone, Vols 5 and 20.* The Queen's University, Belfast

Ferry, D. (Trans) *Horace the Odes* Bilingual Ed. Farrar, Straus & Giroux, New York (1997)

Gamble, J. *Views of Society and Manners in the North of Ireland.* London (1819)

Guthrie, W. *Hard Travellin' Ludlow Music.* (1959)

Hazlitt, W. On Going a Journey - from *Table Talk No1.* (1822)

Ledwidge, F. *Songs of the Fields* (1915); *Songs of Peace* (1916); *Last Songs* (1918)

Lewis, S. *Topographical Dictionary of Ireland, Vols I and II* (1837)

Longfellow, H.W. *Haunted Houses – from Birds of Passage* (1858)

Lovell, E.W. *A Green Hill Far Away: A Life of Mrs Cecil Francis Alexander*, Friends of St Columb's Cathedral, Coleraine Printing Co(1994)

McEvoy, J. *Statistical Survey of Tyrone,* Royal Dublin Society (1802)

MacNeice, L. *Collected Poems.* Faber, London (1966)

Mellon, T. *Thomas Mellon and His Times,* University of Pittsburg Press (1994)

Murphy, D. *A Place Apart,* John Murray Ltd. London (1978)

Pigott Directory of Ireland (1824)

Robotham, R. *The Last Years of the Wee Donegal – 1950-59.* Newtownards (1998)

Stevenson R.L *Travels with a Donkey in the Cevennes, in Journeys,* (ed) Charles Nicholl Dent, London(1997)

Dear Reader

This book is from our exciting new range which cover rivers in Ireland and includes:–

By the Banks of the Bann   **The Liffey**
My Lagan Love   **Following the Foyle**

This new range is a development of our much complimented illustrated book series which includes:-

Belfast	Blanchardstown, Castleknock and the Park
By the Lough's North Shore	Dundrum, Stillorgan & Rathfarnham
East Belfast	Blackrock, Dun Laoghaire and Dalkey
South Belfast	Bray and North Wicklow
Antrim, Town & Country	Dublin 4
North Antrim	Limerick's Glory
Across the Roe	Galway on the Bay
Inishowen	Connemara
Donegal Highlands	The Book of Clare
Donegal, South of the Gap	Kildare
Donegal Islands	Carlow
Islands of Connaught	Monaghan
Sligo	Athlone
Mayo	Cavan
North Kerry	Kilkenny
Fermanagh	Armagh
Omagh	Ring of Gullion
Cookstown	Carlingford Lough
Dundalk & North Louth	The Mournes
Drogheda & the Boyne Valley	Heart of Down
Fingal	Strangford's Shores
Dublin's North Coast	Lecale

We can also supply prints, individually signed by the artist, of the paintings featured in many of the above titles as well as many other areas of Ireland.

For the more athletically minded our illustrated walking book series includes:–

Bernard Davey's Mourne   **Tony McAuley's Glens**
Rathlin, An Island Odyssey   **Bernard Davey's Mourne Part 2**

To see our full range of titles please visit www.cottage-publications.com

Cottage Publications

Cottage Publications
is an imprint of
Laurel Cottage Ltd
15 Ballyhay Road
Donaghadee, Co. Down
N. Ireland, BT21 0NG

For details on these superb publications and to view samples of the paintings they contain, you can visit our web site
www.cottage-publications.com
or alternatively you can
contact us as follows:–

Telephone: +44 (0)28 9188 8033
Fax: +44 (0)28 9188 8063